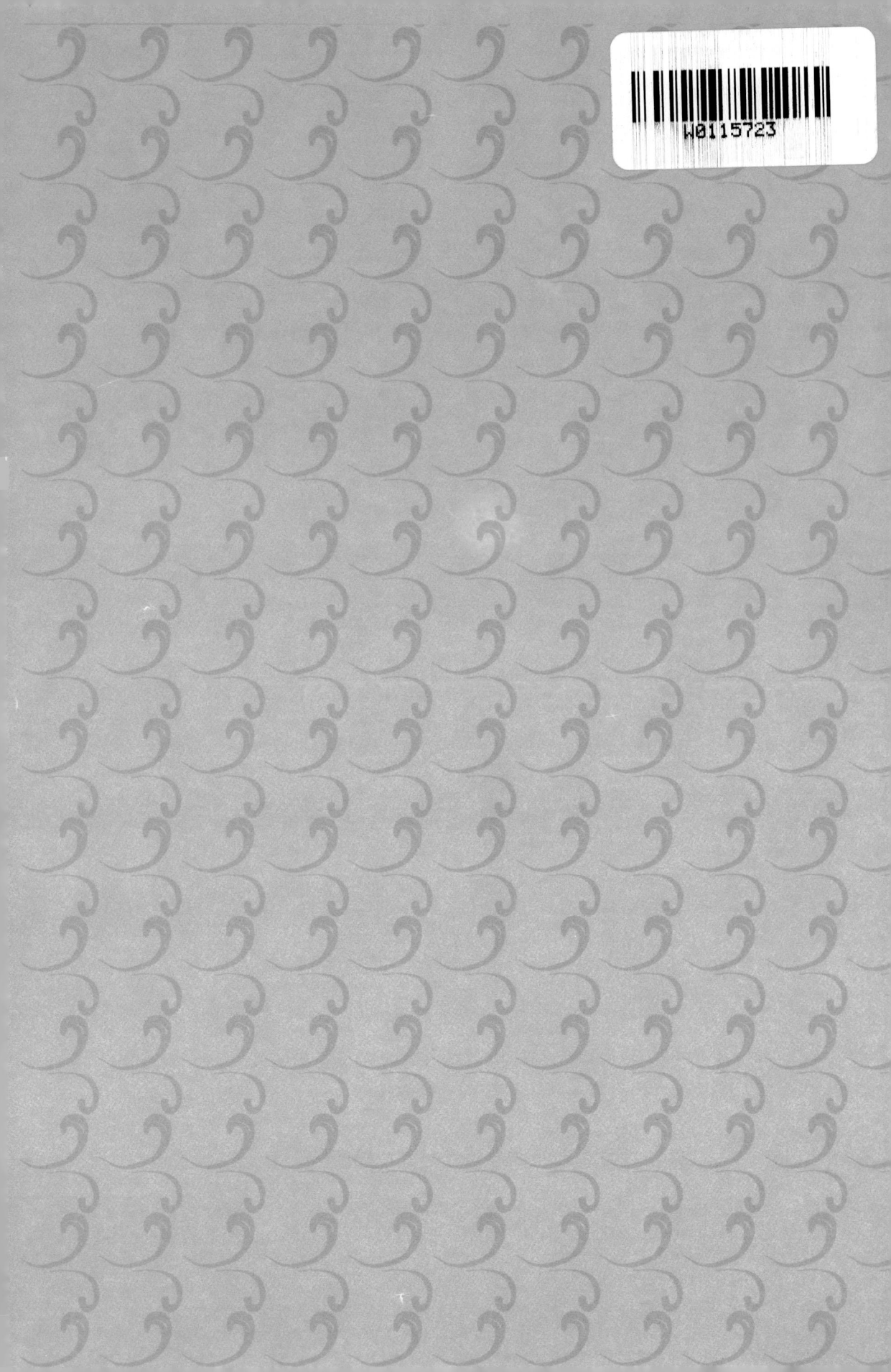

NEW WAYS *for* OLD JUGS

Tradition and Innovation at the Jugtown Pottery

New Ways for Old Jugs
Tradition and Innovation at the Jugtown Pottery

Edited by:

Douglas DeNatale
Jane Przybysz
Jill R. Severn

McKissick Museum
The University of South Carolina
Columbia, South Carolina

Library of Congress Cataloging-In Publication Data

New ways for old jugs: tradition and innovation at the Jugtown
Pottery / edited by Douglas DeNatale, Jane Przybysz, Jill R. Severn.
p. cm.
"Catalog of an exhibition held June 26 to October 23, 1994 at the
McKissick Museum, University of South Carolina, and afterwards at
other museums"—
Includes bibliographical references.
ISBN 0-938983-aa-3 (pbk.)
1. Jugtown pottery—Exhibitions. 2. Jugtown Pottery (Firm)—
Exhibitions. 3. Pottery—20th century—North Carolina—Exhibitions.
I. DeNatale, Douglas, 1953- . II. Przybysz, Jane, 1954- .
III. Severn, Jill R., 1966- . IV. McKissick Museum.
NK4340.J7N48 1994
738.3'09756'352—dc20   94-11701

Photographic Credits

Country Roads, Incorporated, Arlington, Massachusetts, 3b, 9b, 14b, 15a&b, 33, 39, 45, 49, 51, 52, 53
        Photographer Juliana Busbee, 4, 31
        Photographer Valerie Nicholson, 16a, 44

Asia Farlow, 34

Mint Museum of Art, Charlotte, North Carolina
        The Auman Collection, 40

Museum of the City of New York, 91.53.42 Gift of Sonia & Alexander Alland, Jr., New York, New York
        Photographer Jessie Tarbox Beals, 6b

North Carolina Division of Archives and History, Raleigh, North Carolina, 3a, 16b, 46
        Photographer Juliana Busbee, 8
        Photographer Bill Sharpe, 42
        Photographer W. Burden Stage, 27

Ben Owen III
        Photographer Carol Hunter, 68

Lucille H. Owen, 67

Melvin Owens, 9a

Pamela and Vernon Owens, Jugtown Pottery, Seagrove, North Carolina, 2, 24, 56, 60
        Photographer Carol Hunter, 18b, 73a&b
        Photographer Pamela Owens, 43
        Photographer Al Powers, 55
        Photographer Paul Wagnor, 70
        Photographer Jack Sink, 71
        Photographer Janice Hussey, 72

John Garrett Teague, 36

Photographer Charles Tompkins, Washington, Virginia, 17, 59

The Tufts Archives, Pinehurst, North Carolina
        Photographer John Hemmer, 37

UNC Library at Chapel Hill, North Carolina Collection, Chapel Hill, North Carolina
        Photographer Bayard Wooten, 13a&b

The University of South Carolina, Columbia, South Carolina
        McKissick Museum
        Photographer Charles Jackson Barber, Jr., 19
        Photographer Gordon Brown, xii, 6a, 10a&b, 11, 12, 18a, 20a,b&c, 61, 65
        Photographer Hunter Clarkson, Alt-Lee Inc., Columbia, South Carolina, cover, 76, 80, 84, 87, 88, 91

Table of Contents

Foreword

The seed for this project was planted during a casual conversation at the reception following George Holt and Deborah Eagle's wedding at an old farmhouse in Yanceyville, North Carolina. George, the director of the Folklife Section for the North Carolina Arts Council, and Deborah, the design arts coordinator at the Council, had gathered a large group of long-time friends—artists, musicians, folklorists—to celebrate with them. North Carolina traditional artists, among them National Heritage Award winners, rubbed shoulders with revival musicians and avant garde artists. There was a festival air as old friends shared reminiscences to the accompaniment of impromptu string band ensembles.

In the course of one of these conversations, Pam and Vernon Owens, the present-day owners of the Jugtown Pottery, asked me about the series of folklife exhibitions McKissick Museum had developed over the years. They wondered if McKissick would ever be interested in producing an exhibition on Jugtown. My response was positive, but a little guarded. With its striking history in an area of the Southeast now recognized as a center for traditional southern pottery, Jugtown is a compelling topic for a museum exhibition, and—not surprisingly—there had already been several significant exhibitions about Jugtown. At the same time, this seemed an appropriate time to look again at Jugtown, particularly because a concerted effort to establish a museum of North Carolina traditional pottery in Moore County was gaining ground under George's leadership. As I talked over the idea with Pam and Vernon, we were joined by Nancy Sweezy, who had directed Jugtown during the 1970s and early 1980s. Nancy joined her enthusiastic support to the prospect of a new look at Jugtown, and as we talked, the notion of focusing the exhibit on the social history of the pottery emerged.

The human story of Jugtown and its place among the traditional family potteries of Moore County is dramatic and emotionally charged. Jacques and Juliana Busbee, Jugtown's founders, created an enterprise at once commercial, artistic, and social. At its heart was a tension between a regional utilitarian folk tradition and a cosmopolitan decorative arts aesthetic. The Busbees built their enterprise upon a claim for the intrinsic beauty of the utilitarian tradition, and promoted their pottery as a fusion of innate traditional form with their own highly developed artistic sensibilities. Their venture was resoundingly successful, measured by the circle of devoted and passionate supporters drawn to the pottery both during the Busbees' lifetimes and after their deaths.

The human and artistic drama did not end with the Busbees. Jugtown was reborn several times, first under the direction of John Maré, a New York entrepreneur, then under Country Roads, a non-profit organization that supported Nancy Sweezy's reinvigoration of Jugtown, and most recently under Vernon and Pam Owens. Each of these eras had its passionate aficionados and detractors; each era produced its own redaction of "the Jugtown aesthetic."

The interplay of internal and external forces in the evolution of regional culture has received a great deal of attention in recent years, particularly as cultural specialists—applied anthropologists, folklorists, public historians, and ethnomusicologists—grapple with their own roles in the mix of culture. The Jugtown Pottery provides a compelling and instructive example of this interplay in its own rich and at times controversial history. With this exhibition, our intention is to place a number of the issues involved in this interaction before the public, recognizing that the multiple perspectives that have grown from the Busbees' original endeavor demand a fair hearing.

A special debt of gratitude goes to Jill Severn, the curator of this exhibition. Through her extraordinary diligence and intrepid research, Jill has uncovered a tremendous amount of new information concerning the Jugtown story. Her organizational and intellectual skills were put to the test, and amply demonstrated, as she identified and secured artifacts, composed panel and label copy for the exhibition, and assembled the materials for the catalog. This exhibition and catalog simply could not have been accomplished without her.

We hope this exhibition and catalog will provide a new and valuable overview of the legacy of the Jugtown Pottery and its ongoing contribution to the region's cultural heritage.

Dr. Douglas DeNatale
Project Director

Preface

Time changes everything. Like many aphorisms, this often repeated phrase contains a powerful truth. It speaks of a longing for things past while recognizing the progressive spirit. While it is this progressive spirit that has fundamentally transformed American culture and custom since at least the middle of the nineteenth century, we cling to the desire to retain and remember the traditional. Also buried somewhere in time are the elusive truths of historical accuracy.

Often organized for the expressed purpose of preserving the past, museums are constantly dealing with how to represent not only that past, but the forces that initiate, propel and constrain change. *New Ways for Old Jugs: Tradition and Innovation at the Jugtown Pottery* proved to be a challenging case study. How does a museum reconstruct and interpret the seventy-year history of one North Carolina pottery?

McKissick has a solid reputation within the museum field for its thorough commitment to enhancing the public's understanding and appreciation of cultural traditions in the Southeast. Jugtown ware, Catawba Indian pottery and alkaline-glazed stoneware join seagrass and split-oak baskets and piecework quilts as prominent holdings within the Museum's collections. But more important than the preservation of objects for future generations to behold is McKissick's ability to research and document the social history of the people and traditions that generated them.

The Museum first considered doing an exhibition on Jugtown because the Pottery evolved from a commitment to preserving traditional craft practices at a time when the industrialization of ceramic production had made many of these practices irrelevant. Jugtown was also an appropriate topic because it successfully reshaped some local practices by employing a fine art aesthetic and forms borrowed from other sources to produce pottery that would appeal to the tastes of an urban middle-class market.

What started out as a simple exploration of the history of one small pottery soon expanded into an intricate investigation of the making, marketing and collecting of Southern Craft in general. Southern Craft has become a national consumer item—pre-packaged and stereotyped. By looking at how notions of authenticity, tradition, and the South have figured in the many incarnations of Jugtown, this exhibition invites the viewer to consider the complex processes by which various forms of community-based cultural production are perpetuated, revived and reinvented. As with Jugtown, it is largely through stories that makers and collectors, insiders and outsiders, communities and culture workers explain to themselves and to others why they do what they do. Because of this, the exhibition and catalogue document their subject through the objects, images and words of many of the participants in Jugtown Pottery's history. As the curator states, "They have invoked the concept of 'tradition' for many different purposes and with remarkably varied results."

Lynn Robertson
Executive Director

Acknowledgements

When I began working at McKissick Museum, I had hoped to participate in the research for its exhibition on African American celebrations. African American cultural history had been the focus of my research as a graduate student in the history program at the University of Georgia. To my initial dismay, I learned I would be working instead on something called Jugtown Pottery. Soon after beginning the research for this project, however, my dismay quickly evaporated. I became thoroughly absorbed by the fascinating history of the Pottery.

Throughout the years of its operation, the Jugtown Pottery has been part of many of the events and ideas that have shaped what the South means to both southerners and non-southerners. Beginning with the Busbee era of operation, Jugtown was a much publicized locus for the revival of southern rural handicrafts. Again in the 1960s, Jugtown was an important point of convergence for the folk revival movement that captured the imaginations of many young people.

Like the other distinctive parts of the South, such as Appalachia and the Lowcountry, Jugtown is much more than just a place. It is an imaginative world created and recreated over the years of its operation by its owners, its workers, and its patrons. With such a wide and varied group of participants there are many different stories of Jugtown to tell. Through this catalog and exhibition, it has been McKissick's aim to represent this rich variety of perspectives.

This endeavor would not have been possible without the tremendous generosity of so many people who contributed to the research and production of this exhibit. Like most exhibitions, *New Ways for Old Jugs* is not the product of McKissick Museum alone, but the collaborative effort of many individuals and institutions.

Often, when one begins researching a subject, the chief stumbling block is a lack of information; for the Jugtown project the problem was precisely the opposite. There were hundreds of newspaper articles, speeches and letters written by many of the key figures associated with Jugtown over the years, all of which told a slightly different story. Excavating the layers of these memories was a challenge. But ultimately, what was revealed provides a much richer picture of Jugtown's history.

Several individuals deserve special thanks for their expert assistance in this task. The consultants for this project—Dr. Charles G. Zug III, of the University of North Carolina at Chapel Hill, Dr. Leonidas J. Betts, of North Carolina State University, and Pamela and Vernon Owens, of Jugtown Pottery—have far exceeded their responsibility to this project. All have generously offered their knowledge of Jugtown both formally in interviews published in this catalog, and informally, through countless telephone conversations and written correspondence. During the initial planning phase of the project, Dr. Zug and Dr. Betts provided their invaluable expertise in the area of North Carolina traditional pottery. Dr. Betts and Pamela and Vernon Owens cheerfully made their significant collections of Jugtown pottery available for the exhibition. A special note of appreciation is due to Pamela and Vernon Owens whose patience with my frequent questions about Jugtown and requests for their time has been boundless.

Dr. Douglas DeNatale was responsible for the initial conceptualization and development of this exhibit. He served as the project's director and wrote "New Ways for Old Jugs: Tradition and Innovation at the Jugtown Pottery," an essay published in this exhibition catalog. His essay clarifies many of the significant moments of Jugtown's history and presents the variety of perspectives of persons associated with that history. Sally Council performed exceptional work for this exhibition, identifying and interviewing many of the key people associated with Jugtown. She brought her own considerable knowledge of North Carolina pottery and sensitivity as an ethnographer to this task. Nancy Sweezy also assisted the project in several important ways. She offered her considerable knowledge of Jugtown gleaned through both her own research and her direct participation at the Pottery as its director from 1968 through 1983. Acting on behalf of Country Roads, Ms. Sweezy permitted McKissick to borrow several significant artifacts associated with Jugtown, including a scrapbook begun by Juliana Busbee in the 1920s containing Jugtown photographs, news clippings, and ephemera, and updated in the 1970s by Ms. Sweezy and the apprentices at Jugtown. This scrapbook contains many original photographs and memorabilia that rarely have been publicly viewed. Taken as a whole, the scrapbook is one of the most complete archival resources on Jugtown available. Many of the images in this catalog and in the Jugtown exhibition have been drawn from this scrapbook.

For this project McKissick has relied on individual voices to convey the variety of opinions concerning Jugtown's development and ongoing impact. The Museum is extremely grateful to the individuals who have graciously shared their time and knowledge, and who have allowed us to present their edited testimony in this catalog. We thank Charles G. Zug III, William Arthur Staley, Annie Cagle Teague, John Garrett Teague, Lucille H. Owen, Melvin L. Owens,

Woodrow Pruett, William Bridges, Louise Cox, Joanne Bluethenthal, William Moore, Joe Wilkinson, Nancy Sweezy, Leonidas Betts, Ben Owen III, Pamela Owens, and Vernon Owens. Special thanks to Joanne Bluethenthal for allowing McKissick to borrow her collection of pamphlets and news clippings associated with Jugtown, and to Woodrow Pruett and William Bridges for lending their wonderful collection of letters written to them by their dear friend, Juliana Busbee.

New Ways for Old Jugs has had the luxury of building upon the research of a number of institutions and individual scholars. Jean Crawford's *Jugtown Pottery: History and Design* has been an invaluable source of information on Jugtown during the Busbee period of operation. Its bibliography of archival and published material laid the groundwork for McKissick's own research. Similarly, the North Carolina Museum of Art's catalog and exhibition, *Jugtown Pottery: The Busbee Vision* by Gay Mahaffey Hertzman offered an insightful view of the aesthetic sensibilities which guided the Busbees in the creation of the vocabulary of Jugtown pottery forms. Charles Zug's *Turners and Burners: The Folk Potters of North Carolina* was the chief reference for information concerning the history of the larger pottery tradition in North Carolina, of which Jugtown was a part. Nancy Sweezy's *Raised in Clay: The Southern Pottery Tradition* provided an excellent overview of many of the folk potters still turning in North Carolina and the Southeast.

William Moore of the Greensboro Museum, Jai Jordan of the Mint Museum, Janis Pardue of the Walter Clinton Jackson Library at the University of North Carolina in Greensboro, Sally Peterson of the North Carolina Museum of History, Jan Ramirez of the Museum of the City of New York, David Dearinger of the National Academy of Design, Lawrence Campbell of the Art Student's League, Susan Taylor of Salem Academy and College, Anne Brennan of St. John's Museum of Art, Charlotte Brown and Lisa Kessler of the Visual Arts Center of North Carolina State University, Christine Thompson of St. Mary's Junior College Library, Elizabeth Reid Murray, and Ray Owen of Moore County Historical Association were most generous in providing historical and artifactual information. A special note of gratitude to Ray Owen for all of his tireless assistance in locating significant pieces of Jugtown pottery as well as individuals knowledgeable about its history.

Several individuals have been particularly helpful in providing images for this exhibit. Jerry Cotten of the Photographic Collection, Wilson Library, University of North Carolina, Steve Massengill of the State of North Carolina Department of Cultural Resources, Archives and Records Section, Khris Januzek of the Tufts Archives of the Given Memorial Library, Leslie Nolan of the Museum of the City of New York, Diana Arecco of the New York Historical Society, Marie Hélène Gold of the Schlesinger Library, and Martha Mayberry of the Mint Museum all offered their considerable knowledge, expertise, and enthusiasm to our efforts to locate images associated with Jugtown Pottery. McKissick

Museum was also fortunate to be able to have access to a number of images from the private collections of Nancy Sweezy/Country Roads, Charles Tompkins, Lucille H. Owen, Ben Owen III, John Garrett Teague, Asia Farlow, Pamela and Vernon Owens, Melvin L. Owens, and Woodrow Pruett and William Bridges. Special thanks to John Garrett Teague and William Reeder for identifying individuals in some of the early photographs taken at Jugtown.

McKissick is grateful to institutions and individuals who have generously loaned pottery and related objects for this exhibition. They are: The Visual Arts Center of North Carolina State University, Moore County Historical Association, The Museum at the Fashion Institute of Technology, The Hambidge Center for Creative Arts and Sciences, Salem Academy and Library, St. John's Museum of Art, Pamela and Vernon Owens, Country Roads, Leonidas J. Betts, Joe Wilkinson, Ray Wilkinson, Anne and Allen Bloom, Stephen and Lala Compton, Charles Tompkins, Peggy and Jack Kenealy, Donald and Betty Morphis, Ben Owen III, Owen Collins, Daniel Ray Owen, William W. Ivey, Charles Jackson Barber, Jr., Judy Mofield Mallow, Vivian Prim Evans, Mark and Yolanda Kutney, and George Viall.

Substantial credit for the success of this exhibition and catalog is due to the hard work and consistent cooperation of the McKissick Museum staff. Jane Przybysz and Lesley Williams of the Folklife and Oral History Section of the Museum were unswerving in their support of the Jugtown exhibition, often placing their own projects on hold in order to provide assistance. Lesley Williams provided indefatigable guidance as the Interim Director of the Folklife and Oral History Section and acted as a liaison for obtaining many of the archival photographs for the exhibition and catalog. Jane Przybysz served as co-editor of the catalog and brought her considerable knowledge of the larger craft revival movement in the South to many rewarding discussions during the conceptualization phase of the Jugtown exhibition. I cannot thank these two individuals enough for their support both tangible and intangible.

Research assistants in the Folklife and Oral History Program, Kristin Jurgens, Catherine Lesesne, Tonya Green, and Angela Houston organized all of the archival materials relating to the Jugtown project, transcribed interviews, and helped to track down innumerable leads. Their spirited teamwork and commitment to the project was a considerable asset.

Carrie Taylor served as coordinator for all in-house black and white photography and handled all the transfers of pieces from McKissick's collection to the exhibition. She also organized and copied much of the archival material obtained for the exhibition. Karen Nickless checked citations for the catalog essay and assisted with the transport of objects from lenders to the Museum.

Catherine Wilson Horne, Director of Development and Public Services, drawing upon her considerable knowledge and expertise, supervised the production schedule of the exhibition. Peggy Nunn, Administrative Assistant, coordinated the text production for the catalog and was an invaluable resource for questions concerning style. Carol Copeland, Assistant to the Vice Provost and Dean for Library and Information Systems, transcribed many of interviews for the catalog.

The educational programs and materials associated with this exhibition were developed and produced by Deanna Kerrigan, Curator of Educational Services.

McKissick Museum's exhibition and graphic designers, Lyn Bell Rose and Tracey Thompson, designed and oversaw production of the exhibition and catalog. They were ably assisted by museum technicians G. Micheal Bagwell, Stuart Heebner, and Dennis Durham. Special thanks to Micheal Bagwell and Stuart Heebner, who handled the packing of objects for transport to the Museum. Micheal Bagwell also completed the condition reports for the objects in the exhibit. Curator of Exhibitions Alice Bouknight arranged the regional traveling schedule for the exhibition, and on several occasions took time out from her already busy schedule to pick up objects for the exhibition. Gordon Brown provided excellent photographic support for the exhibition and the catalog.

I would like to thank Lynn Robertson. As the director of McKissick Museum she continues to be a strong and enthusiastic supporter of research and public education programs like the Jugtown project. Special appreciation is also due the University of South Carolina for its continued commitment to McKissick Museum and all of its programs.

Finally, McKissick Museum is grateful to the Folk Arts Program of the National Endowment for the Arts and to the Folklife Section of the North Carolina Arts Council for the support that has made this project possible. The Museum would like to thank George Holt, Wayne Martin, Beverly Patterson, and Sylvia Saavedra of the North Carolina Arts Council, and Dan Sheehy and Barry Bergey of the National Endowment for the Arts, Folk Arts Program for their invaluable assistance with this project.

Jill Severn
Project Curator

Lead-glazed earthenware pie plate from Randolph County, North Carolina, ca. last quarter of 19th century. Maker unknown.
Collection of William W. Ivey.

New Ways for Old Jugs:
Tradition and Innovation at the Jugtown Pottery

Douglas DeNatale

Founded in 1921 by Jacques and Juliana Busbee, the Jugtown Pottery of Moore County, North Carolina, was a self-conscious attempt to revive the local traditional pottery industry by introducing forms, glazes, and techniques from other pottery traditions that were yet consonant with local tradition. Jugtown achieved wide renown, and has been sometimes credited—and as often discredited—with rescuing the local pottery tradition. What happened at Jugtown was a localized, and special case of interaction between an existing cultural process and outsiders seeking to influence that process, a form of interaction that David Whisnant has termed "cultural intervention."[1] The Jugtown enterprise was connected to a larger crafts revival that occurred throughout the Southeast during the early twentieth century, yet its story diverges from that larger cultural movement in a number of important and revealing ways. Significantly, there was not one, but at least two phases of cultural intervention at Jugtown, first under the Busbees from 1917 until the 1950s, and later under Country Roads, a non-profit organization that ran the pottery from 1968 to 1983. The manner in which the Jugtown story unfolded is an intriguing example of the processes that create cultural traditions and cultural understandings.

Here is a version of the Jugtown origin story that became more or less normative during the Busbees' lifetimes:

While visiting the 1915 Davidson County Fair in Lexington, North Carolina, in her role as chair of the Art Department of the North Carolina Federation of Women's Clubs, Juliana Busbee was invited to help arrange a display of fruit. She asked for a tin plate from the local hardware store, and instead was brought a bright orange clay pie plate, or what locals called a dirt dish. So enraptured was she by the plate's innate beauty, that she immediately abandoned her duties and rushed to the store to buy a sample of every piece of pottery available. There she learned that the pottery came from Moore County. She shipped her clothes home by parcel post and filled her suitcase with the pottery. When Jacques met her at Union Station in Raleigh, the couple unpacked the pottery on the station floor in their zeal to examine it.

Seized with a new mission, the Busbees set out to discover the maker. Jacques wrote to the "mayor" of each borough in Moore County, and eventually learned that the pottery came from the settlement of Whynot. By this time, the Busbees were spending the winter of 1917 in New York City. But when Jacques had to return to Raleigh on business, he planned a trip to Whynot. Upon disembarking from the

train in Seagrove, the nearest train station, Jacques was marked as a "furriner" by the New York labels on his suitcase and his upper-middle-class accent. The locals suspected him of being a German spy, particularly when they saw the packages of sample glazes in his suitcase. Nonetheless, Jacques managed to make his way to the few remaining local potters, who were barely clinging to their way of life. Through later research, Jacques would discover these men to be direct descendants of a continuous line of potters from Staffordshire, England, who had emigrated to Moore County in 1750. Dedicated to the revival of this important vernacular art, the Busbees sold their Raleigh home and library. Juliana moved to New York to start a tearoom in Greenwich Village, through which she marketed the pottery, and Jacques returned to Moore County to work with the young Ben Owen to create translations of pure, early oriental forms in native clay. With Juliana's marketing expertise and Jacques's artistic genius, the Busbees single-handedly rescued the North Carolina pottery tradition.

By no means could this distilled version of the story be considered authoritative. As it was reported in period newspapers and in the various personal accounts the Busbees gave of their project, factual contradictions, shadings of motives, and biographical details varied. A critical biography of the Busbees remains to be written.[2] Yet even a cursory examination of documentary sources provides a basis for reinterpreting the Busbees' own account of their history.

James Littlejohn Busbee was born in 1870 to a distinguished Raleigh family. His father Charles, grandfather Perrin, and great-grandfather Johnson each had been prominent lawyers in North Carolina, and his grandmother had been the daughter of North Carolina Attorney General James F. Taylor. But James departed from his family's accustomed occupational path when he left the Horner Military Academy in Oxford, North Carolina, in 1889 to study art in New York City.[3] James attended classes at the National Academy of Design, the Arts Students' League, and the Chase School.[4] At the National Academy, James enrolled in the Antique Class from 1889 to 1893, but failed to qualify. He also enrolled in the Academy's Painting Class and Life Class. He apparently studied sculpture under Augustus Saint-Gaudens, as well as classical painting under John Henry Twachtman at the Art Students' League. He pursued his art studies in New York at least until 1897. In 1891, after two years of formal art training, James had apparently absorbed the bohemian atmosphere of the city thoroughly, for in that year he adopted the artistic name "Jacques," by which he was known for the rest of his life.[5] Around the turn of the century, Jacques began returning

James Littlejohn Busbee, ca. 1890s.

paintings, Jacques embarked upon an exhibition and lecture tour within the state, delivering an oratorical discourse on the early colonization attempt while displaying each painting in turn. "Mr. Busbee gives a splendid condensed story of the Lost Colony in his lecture," reported a Hickory, North Carolina, newspaper in 1911 after Jacques's appearance there: "He has thoroughly mastered this epoch in our history and one follows him with unflagging interest until the end. Some of his descriptions showed him to be as great a word painter as he is with brush and palette."[10] Jacques seems to have been encouraged by the audience response, for he published a number of articles on coastal North Carolina in several periodicals. When the Busbee ancestral home in Raleigh was torn down in 1914, *The News and Observer* noted of its owner, "Mr. Jacques Busbee, artist and writer, who with pen and with brush, has done much to bring the Eastern coast of North Carolina into prominence, is one of the third generation to be born in this house. Hatteras, the life savers, and the shore folk have been his themes. But he has the sentiment for Raleigh, and feeling for the place that has been the home of his life. And now it must go."[11]

Busbee's articles on the shore folk appealed to a burgeoning fascination among North Carolina's middle-class urbanites for the apparent survival of ancient customs and lore in isolated rural populations. Among present-day inhabitants of Hatteras Island, in whose faces he saw marks of Indian ancestry commingled with English features, he thought he had found the descendants of the Lost Colony of Roanoke. "Then, you will note the use of many obsolete words and phrases," he brought forth as further evidence, "old English of Chaucer's time, quaint turns of expression, words used with a significance they had long ago, but now spoken with a modern meaning."[12]

On a national level, this amateur antiquarian impulse had begun to be formalized among scholars such as Harvard University's Francis James Child and George Lyman Kittredge as the study of folklore. The systemized collection of oral lore by a network of enthusiastic laypeople spread South in the first years of the new century. In North Carolina, a statewide effort to collect oral folklore was organized by Professor Frank C. Brown upon his arrival at Duke University in 1909.[13]

Jacques's writings were formed within this burgeoning interest in a cultural "other," or folk, whose lifeways could be seen as exotic and familiar at the same time. In this, and in his desire to recreate his own life as a bohemian artist, Jacques Busbee found a kindred spirit in Julia Adeline Royster. Also a member of Raleigh's upper-middle-class, she had evinced an interest in the lore of the folk as early as

periodically to his native North Carolina in search of commissions for portrait and landscape paintings. Judging from the Busbees' later accounts, it must have been a heart-breaking undertaking. "Portrait painting in North Carolina is close akin to the mortician," reflected Juliana in 1929.[6] Ten years later, she would remember, "We were frightfully bored with painting portraits no one liked & landscapes that no one would buy."[7] Jacques must have used all of his family connections to secure commissions. A 1906 letter to North Carolina Chief Justice Walter Clark is probably typical:

> *Raleigh N C*
> *Sept 5*
>
> *Hon Walter Clark*
> *Dear Sir:*
> *You gave me an order for a portrait of Mrs. Clark last winter—but could not decide on the photo from which you wanted it done. Have you ever come to any decision or have you decided not to have it done at all?*
> *I am back in my studio after a summer in New York & should you still desire to have this portrait done I should be glad to do it for you now. Please let me know.*
>
> *Yrs truly*
> *Jacques Busbee* [8]

It may also have been family connections that secured Jacques a commission from the North Carolina Historical Commission in 1907 to paint a series of historical paintings depicting the first settlement of the North Carolina coast for the Jamestown Exposition. He apparently spent a number of months on Roanoke Island and the Outer Banks while he completed this series of fourteen paintings.[9] This was to be the only major commission of Jacques's life as a painter. Yet the success Jacques enjoyed from its accomplishment was more literary than painterly. After completing the series of

1907, when she collected an African American funeral song she later submitted to Professor Brown of Duke. Recounting that experience in 1915, she wrote to Brown:

I have done much illustrating for magazines and have rather specialized on our old-time darkey— Uncle Ananias was one of my most delightful models. Several years ago he died. His wife, Aunt Mity Ann, urged me to attend the funeral… I wish I could tell you all this— my right hand won't convey my knowledge of that wonderful orgy.

The sermon was astounding. This song was made up then and there by the preacher, and was lined out to the congregation, who moaned and sang it with every possible Methodist quaver (I'm one myself). There were many more verses. I wrote down all that I could remember, at the time. I have some very good pictures of the old man. They're yours if you want them.[14]

Jacques and Juliana Busbee with their dog in front of their cabin at Jugtown, 1938.

Julia Adeline Royster, ca. 1890s.

Coming from the same social milieu, Julia Royster had probably known Jacques Busbee from childhood. By 1908, she already had changed her own name to the more artistic Juliana.[15] As her letter to Frank C. Brown hinted, Juliana also had begun to pursue a professional career in photography, which she apparently had studied under a relative at St. Mary's Junior College in Raleigh.[16] Like her lifelong friend,

photographer Bayard Wooten, Juliana encountered enormous social obstacles to her dream of becoming a professional photographer. A shared aesthetic sensibility in the face of social skepticism seems also to have been an important element of her relationship with Jacques Busbee. When the two were married in 1910, their respective, respectable families seem to have been a little nonplussed by the unconventional couple. According to Juliana, "My family, the Busbee family, all our friends and relatives forecast tragedy for the two J's. We had to make a success of our marriage—and did, to their dismay."[17]

In her own later writing, Juliana consistently elevated her husband's artistic vision and practical drive, without entirely discounting her own acumen. Yet, all evidence indicates that it was Juliana who played the major role in laying the groundwork for the creation of Jugtown. This was not the discovery of a moment, but a prolonged personal journey.

That journey may have begun in 1908, when Juliana's name first appeared on the rolls of the Raleigh Woman's Club. Within her own social set, and indeed throughout the South, the women's club movement would have a considerable impact on social and political life. Juliana's mother, aunt, and sisters were founding members of the Raleigh chapter, as was Jacques's sister, Louise. Though their emerging social critique remained wholly within the gender constraints of their own social universe, the club members debated social reform issues ranging from child labor to suffrage, and actively sought to influence family members who were political and business leaders. Juliana's own participation appears to have been restricted to artistic activities considered appropriate to women's sphere. Two years after joining the club's Art Department in 1909, she became department chair. Within the framework of the club, she found space to become engaged with a cultural sphere beyond her own. "Helping our rural people who have no profession, to help themselves, is the interpretation of Social Service that our Art Department wish[es] to give," wrote Juliana in a speech from this period.

> Surely the watch words of the Club Women are Love & Service. Not until every one realises the joy & beauty & dignity of service will the full meaning of Life be revealed to us. Every gifted person realises his or her great obligation to God, & the only way that obligation can be squared is by sharing freely with the less fortunate.[18]

While chair of the Raleigh Woman's Club Art Department, Juliana seized upon handicraft as the frame in which social service and art could be merged. "The motto of the art department of the club for this year, 'Pictures are not all of art', has been clearly demonstrated in the work of the department," declared a club newspaper in 1914. "In fact a large part of the club seems basket crazy. A number of pretty reed and raffia things have not only been made in the club, but the nurses at the State Hospital have been given enough instruction to begin the work with the patients at the hospital."[19]

The hospital basketry class fit the social mission of the club perfectly. Two years after its inception, Juliana reflected:

> It was beautiful to see what it meant to the patients. We invited the nurses there to come to our club meetings each week where basketry was taught, and then several women from our Dept. would go the Hospital once a week & together we started an Arts & Crafts department. Any one who is interested will notice the exhibit at the State Fair made by the patients. The work is crude, of course, for there is no one to direct

them along lines of [art]—but a good beginning has been made.[20]

Impressed by her efforts, the State Federation of Women's Clubs appointed Juliana chair of the state Art Department in 1915.[21]

As state chair, Juliana worked diligently to expand the handicraft mission. "Our Convention decided that the only art that could reach all of our state, the poor & the wealthy, the learned and the ignorant was the art of handicraft," she reported.[22] Her state committee, consisting of May Davis and Mrs. George Summey of Raleigh, Mrs. T. L. Bayne of Manchester, Bayard Wooten of New Bern, and Mattie Dowd of Charlotte, offered a lecture/demonstration series to local club chapters in the areas of basketry, weaving, North Carolina pottery, modern landscape, household art, architecture, picture interpretation, and art in child life.[23] "I have spent now 18 months teaching native basketry wherever I could find people who were interested," reported Juliana about this time. "With the help of my wonderful convention we have taught over 2000 women & children, and we know definitely of more than $500. that has been made."[24] As an example of a success story, she cited the case of a "girl of seventeen with average ability" who "had false ideas of life instilled into her by a mother who had lost her wealth and refused to become adjusted to this new age of democracy & feminine independence." "The only money that these two people have had to live on," Juliana continued, "has been the money made by this girl from baskets she has sold."[25] Juliana's fellow committee member, Mrs. T. L. Bayne, organized a similar statewide effort to teach handweaving, and reported that "among the women of our state who have profited by her original ideas is Mrs. A. L. Mast who has woven for the White House, and has gained wide recognition."[26]

This photograph was included in Juliana Busbee's article on pine needle baskets and pottery published in *Everywoman's Magazine*, in 1916. The pottery shows the types of wares that attracted the Busbees when they first began collecting, including the famous pie plate. The original caption reads: "1, Mat glaze, by Mr. C. L. Ryman at Skyland; 2, Candle Stick, Soft Green Mat glaze, by Mr. Ryman; 3, Unglazed Terra Cotta, Made at Weaverville by Mr. George Donkel; 4, 5, 6, 7, Beautiful Specimens of Mr. Bachelder's Work, Made at Candler, N. C.; 10, Unglazed, and Iridescent With Mica, From Franklin County; 11, Jam Pot, Designed by Mrs. Jacques Busbee for the North Carolina Canning Clubs." Photographer was probably Juliana Busbee, ca. 1915.

Jugtown was born in this context of cultural intervention for social uplift, not in the momentary discovery of the fateful pie plate as the Busbees would later claim. The initial date of the Busbees' involvement with traditional North Carolina pottery has yet to be established, but an article published by Juliana in 1916 in the *Everywoman's Magazine* demonstrates that the Busbees' project extended over a prolonged period of time, and began at an earlier date than is generally assumed. "For years Mr. Busbee and I have been collecting specimens from the different potters in the State," wrote Juliana in that article:

> We have drawn designs for the men who have
> grasped the artistic possibilities of their craft.
> Perhaps one of the most beautiful days I ever
> spent was at the kiln of Mr. Wade Johnson in
> Catawba county. Mr. Johnson lives in a
> neighborhood called "Jugtown," where churns,
> pickle jars and crocks of all sorts are made.
> We could see at once the quality of his work,
> and that, with a little guidance along artistic
> lines, his work might be vastly improved. We
> drew some designs for floor vases and umbrella
> stands. The specimens he made for us from
> these designs have attracted a great deal of
> attention from people all over the United
> States who are connoisseurs of pottery.[27]

According to the article, Johnson, a Catawba Valley potter working in the alkaline glaze tradition, was the first potter with whom the Busbees worked. He was followed by C. P. Ryman, whose Nonconnah Pottery in Skyland was produced by turner Walter Stephens, and by Oscar Louis Bachelder of Candler. Photographs illustrating the article also included work by George Donkel of Weaverville and a Mrs. Owl of Yellow Hill, North Carolina. In later discussions of Jugtown history, Ryman and Bachelder retained passing mention, but the interaction with Johnson would be forgotten.

The 1916 article is of particular note because several elements of the later story are present, including the name "Jugtown" and the Busbees' artistic reinterpretation of traditional forms. But in the light of the later story, these elements seem curiously refracted. Judging from this early article, the Busbees' initial interest was sparked by "native" pottery, but they did not seem to attach any great significance to the intrinsic qualities of traditional pottery as they did later at Jugtown. Instead, they stressed the pottery's marketability: "It would be a good investment for some merchant in every town in the State to handle our native pottery. Every tourist wants something characteristic of a place for a souvenir, and what could be more charming than a piece of real North Carolina dirt?" Also present was the famous pie plate, depicted in a photograph accompanying the article, and mentioned in the text, but with considerably less emphasis than it would receive later on: "One of the loveliest things I have," reported Juliana, "is a brilliant orange plate with flecks of wonderful green here and there

on it. Had it been brought from Brittany, it would be thought a museum specimen, but coming from Randolph County, and being a pie plate that costs ten cents, it is not very popular. Those who know its humble origin think it a huge joke on me. But just let me show it to an outsider who is interested in pottery and who knows a thing or two, and I have to keep a watchful eye upon it."[28]

The active interaction between the Busbees and local potters during the period of Juliana's chairmanship of the Art Department is further documented in oral tradition. According to Melvin Owens, whose father J. H. Owen was one of the first potters in Moore County to work with the Busbees, Jacques had previously attempted to work with a member of the Fox family in Chatham County prior to his arrival in Seagrove in 1917. This is corroborated by a 1927 article, which identified the first potter that Jacques worked with as "old Jimmy Fox, the star potter of the section," incorrectly placing Fox in Moore County.[29] Beyond this, Jacques's entry into Moore County may well have preceeded the 1917 German spy story. In his 1929 letter to *The News and Observer*, Jacques stated, "Between the time of our first visits some eight or ten years before, and our return in 1917 there was woeful falling off in the quality as well as the output" of Moore County pottery.[30]

If the Busbees did attempt to influence North Carolina pottery prior to Jugtown, the character of their engagement with potters might be glimpsed in Juliana's discussion of her interaction with O. L. Bachelder. "In 1914, I was Chairman of Art in the Raleigh Woman's Club," she reported in a 1941 letter:

> About that time, I saw a notice in an Asheville
> paper that a potter in Luther was doing nice
> crocks, churns, and flowerpots. We were trying
> to locate all the potters and weavers in the State,
> so I went up to Asheville to see what kind of
> work this potter was doing. I took the train one
> cold morning in March, 1914, and arrived at
> Candler. Here I was first introduced to O. L.
> Bachelder. I spent the day with him, returning
> at night to Asheville; I returned the next day
> and the next. At that time, he had made no
> attempt to do any kind of pottery save
> stoneware.
>
> For those three days, I stood by the wheel and
> had him do for me certain things I wanted, a
> tea set, a lid pitcher, some mugs and plates, a
> salad bowl, some flower bowls, and some little
> jam pots that I wanted the Home Demonstration
> Clubs to use as official containers. He was
> interested and promised to supply duplicate
> things if anyone wanted them. Seeing a copy of
> Omar Khayyám on his table, I suggested that
> as his trade name, and I did his monogram
> which he used as his trademark. I had an

interesting three days. He was a good cook, made all his own bread, baked beans, etc.

That spring, I was elected State Chairman of Art in the North Carolina Federated Club. I saw to it that Mr. Bachelder's work was exhibited all over our State. I sent the things he had done for me from the ocean to the extreme west part of the State so that he quickly became known in North Carolina. We gave him premiums at our State Fair.

I have now the teapot, a pitcher, several plates and mugs, three bowls, two jam pots, and a vase which were made for me by Mr. Bachelder.[31]

These items are pictured in Juliana's 1916 *Everywoman's Magazine* article, and stand somewhere between traditional utilitarian forms and the later oriental redactions created in the collaboration between Jacques and the Jugtown potters.

The Busbees' pre-Jugtown involvement with pottery bears a direct relationship to the early work of cultural missionaries at work in the Southern Highlands. In later public presentations, Juliana demonstrated familiarity with the work of pioneers in this movement such as Eleanor Vance, Charlotte Yale, and Frances Goodrich. "At the time of my keen interest," she reported later, "when I was doing club work, Miss Vance

Albany slip glaze stoneware vase with three handles made by Oscar Louis Bachelder, Candler, North Carolina, ca. early 1920s. Collection of George Viall.

and Miss Yale now of Tryon were doing exquisite work under the patronage of Mrs. Geo. Vanderbilt."[32] It was in the framework of placing native work before a larger audience that Juliana presented her reasons for going to New York to her fellow club members:

For the rest of my term of office I am going to find a market for our workers by bringing work before the people of New York. I shall endeavor to find a place for our native Basket and native Pottery in the expensive Gift & Craft Shops of New York City, where large prices can be obtained.[33]

However, the Busbees seem to have had little subsequent involvement with the mountain craft revival, with the significant exception of their lifelong friendship with Mary Hambidge. Hambidge, the widow of Yale art historian Jay Hambidge, shared the Busbees' emphasis on the spiritual and aesthetic qualities of craft in her work reviving weaving in Rabun Gap, Georgia. Hambidge synthesized a number of classical influences with southern domestic weaving, formulated according to her late husband's principles of dynamic symmetry. From handwoven cloth, she fashioned high-style women's clothing sold through upscale New

"Alice Sit by the Fire": Interior of The Village Store with owner, Alice Palmer, Greenwich Village, N.Y., ca. 1917. The Village Store was later taken over by Juliana Busbee as an outlet for North Carolina handicrafts. The pine needle baskets, under the table and below the shelves suggest that this shop may have been one of the gift and craft shops where Juliana first tried to market North Carolina baskets and pottery when she moved to New York around 1917.

York department stores. Hambidge's clothes were a favorite of Juliana's, who bartered Jugtown pottery for them.

Diverging from the social emphasis of the mountain craft revivalists, the Busbees' focus on aesthetics was the true starting point of Jugtown. In this aspect, their later accounts of Jugtown's origins have some validity. When the Busbees departed for New York City in the winter of 1916, bringing with them their collection of North Carolina crafts, they were motivated in part by the social mission of the Women's Club's Art Department, but they were also fueled by their own longing for the bohemian artistic life of Greenwich Village. "Those who most regret their going will, however, envy them their winter in New York," reported the Raleigh paper, "it being their intention to take an apartment in that part of the city where artists and writers do most congregate and live in an atmosphere far removed from the mean and sordid things of a strenuous commercial world."[34]

What exactly happened next is unclear. According to Juliana's sister club woman Susan Iden, Jacques's return to Moore County was a logical response to a receptive market:

> It was hard at that time to get North Carolina sufficiently enthusiastic over the pottery to put it on the market, so when they went to New York to live shortly afterward, Mr. and Mrs. Busbee took some ware with them. Their New York visitors became enthusiastic, wondering if it were Mexican or Belgium ware; wanted to know all about where it was made and if it could be bought.
>
> It was then that the Busbees conceived the idea of selling the pottery. Somewhere around Why Not, a little cross roads center near the edge of Randolph and Moore counties, they had been told the pottery was made.
>
> "Well, 'why not'," they questioned, and Mr. Busbee packed his trunk and set out for his native State to find the home of the red ware.[35]

As Juliana explained years later, accounting for the apparent casualness with which the couple began their venture, "My husband thought if he could find the potter who made the pie plate—give him the address of some wholesalers in N.Y., that his obligation would have been fulfilled."[36]

Yet something else happened in New York to the Busbees. As Juliana later recalled, "We went to N.Y. for a year and became violent converts to modern art."[37] This was the era of Gertrude Vanderbilt Whitney's Greenwich Village studio, and the birth of the circle of modern artists who brought the European discovery of primitive art to America. The modernists had only just begun to discover the primitive in American decoys, weathervanes, and paintings. The first exhibit of American folk art would not be held at the Whitney Studio Club until 1924.[38] Arriving into such a

milieu at this opportune moment, the Busbees may well have been taken aback by the enthusiasm with which their collection of North Carolina pottery and crafts were received. "The specimens in our collections of this folk craft-pottery which we brought to New York, created such enthusiasm among the artists and ceramic experts who saw it," stated Jacques.[39] Juliana remembered:

> It seems strange, doesn't it—to have one's whole life, and the lives of an entire community, turned upside down by a Pie Plate. And an empty one at that. But the color of it was not drab, even if it was empty.
>
> I found the plate at a county fair—and even though I lost my head, I found a fresh enthusiasm. After all, isn't modern art just that—losing one's head? Haven't artists been using their intellects instead of their eye sight? As I understand it, the modern trend of art is the impulse to wipe the retina clean—thereby seeing things as they are objectively instead of being influenced by the art critics, & seeing as instructed by them for hundreds of years.
>
> It was that idea we gathered from going to many exhibitions of modern art. Fraternizing with the art exponents & the new movement, some 20 years ago, clarified in our minds our attitudes toward our country crafts. We came to see them as a modern primitive expression. After we perceived that idea, life held nothing for us but to see the thing through in our own native land, in our own artist way.[40]

That resolve likely solved many of the personal and artistic tensions the Busbees must have been feeling. Trained in the classical mode, Jacques's own painting would have seemed hopelessly out of touch with the modernists, but in their discovery of the primitive, the Busbees found themselves on the cutting edge.

It may get closer to the truth to assert that the Busbees did not, in fact, discover their orange pie plate at a North Carolina county fair, but among the modern artists of Greenwich Village, who gave the Busbees a new way of seeing the pottery. The pie plate emerged as an icon in their writings for a simple reason: by dating the moment of discovery to an encounter in rural North Carolina, and by locating it within the inherent qualities of a totemic object, their personal story became one of uncovering a wellspring of art in their native state, rather than one of resolving an internal crisis.

The logic of the Busbees' subsequent actions stemmed from the epiphany that allowed them to gain artistic authority over their subject. As an expression of primitive art, the pottery gained its value from a universal impulse that found surviving expression in the Carolina Piedmont, but which

Daniel Craven standing in front of his pottery shop ca. 1915, Moore County, North Carolina. Daniel Craven was one of several Seagrove area potters still making stoneware storage wares when Jacques and Juliana Busbee were traveling around North Carolina collecting handicraft. Indeed, this photograph may have been taken by Juliana.

The literary process by which the Busbees, particularly Juliana, constructed a satisfying history of the Piedmont pottery tradition can be glimpsed in the curious figure of "Old Joe Shuffle," who reappears several times in the evolving account. At the end of the process in 1937, Juliana published "Jugtown Pottery— A New Way for Old Jugs" in the *Bulletin of the American Ceramic Society.*[44] In this version, the following information appears:

Some of the potters, [Jacques] found, had come from Staffordshire, England, about 1740. One old potter whose name was Sheffield (pronounced Shuffle) was a mine of information. Old Joe Shuffle he was called, and the township is named Sheffield, in Moore county—in what the southern part of the county calls the "dark corner." It is in the upper end. Imagine the surprise of finding his name to be Josiah Wedgwood Sheffield! There is a ballad about him too and it goes something like this:

> *"Old Joe Shuffle he kicked a kick wheel,*
> *Old Joe Shuffle turned pots on a wheel,*
> *Old man Shuffle he kicked out a jug,*
> *He drank from it all he could hold."*

The moral of the ballad is that he had delirium tremens and killed his pet drake thinking it was a snake.[45]

had deeper roots. "Perhaps the most amazing thing about this pottery is its close similarity in shape to the pottery of primitive periods in various parts of the earth. But primitiveness is a state of mind, not a point in time nor yet a place," wrote Jacques.[41] The universal plane upon which the Busbees placed their mission from this moment explains both their insistence on the tradition's pedigree, and the casualness with which they manipulated their account. Because they located the authenticity of the traditional object in its inherent artistic nature, the Busbees as artists had the most direct access and the greatest charter for reforming the tradition.

The Busbees claimed to have traced the Moore County tradition through historical records and oral tradition to a Peter Craven, who directly transported the folk pottery tradition from Staffordshire, England, to Moore County in 1750.[42] During his own research on North Carolina's traditional pottery, Charles Zug was unable to substantiate this claim beyond the existence of a Peter Craven who probably came to the area sometime after 1761. Zug notes, "In actuality, the Germans and Moravians appear to have been the first potters in the Piedmont; the Staffordshire connection is tenuous and unproven; and no tax receipt exists to verify Peter's work as a potter." Noting that three of Craven's grandchildren were listed as potters in the documentary record by the early nineteenth century, and that the Cravens would emerge as one of the most important of the potter families in the region, Zug suggests "there may well be a grain of truth" in the Busbees' assertions.[43] That grain was almost certainly polished by the Busbees' artistic imagination.

The story is intriguing on a number of levels. It buttresses the Busbees' claim of Staffordshire ancestry by suggesting a vernacular awareness of that history, as indicated by the survival of the famous English potter Josiah Wedgewood's name in present-day Moore County. The inclusion of the ballad fragment was a second piece of vernacular lore, affirming the Busbees' authority as collectors of oral tradition. As satisfying as the story is, however, it almost certainly was a complete fabrication.

Local Moore County historian R. E. Wicker reported to Jean Crawford, author of the most balanced account of Jugtown, that although there had been Sheffields in the area, none were known to have been potters. "I do not believe this claim can be supported," he wrote in reference to Busbee's assertion that one was named Josiah Wedgewood Sheffield. Furthermore, Boyce Yow "remembered no Sheffields living in this section at the time Mr. Busbee came down."[46] To my knowledge, neither is there any variant of the ballad fragment in any scholarly folklore collection.

James H. Owen transferring moist clay from a mixing box to a pug mill at his own pottery shop in Moore County, N.C., ca. 1920. Though J. H. Owen made wares for the Busbees to sell in New York for several years before his death in 1923, he made all of this pottery at his own shop.

In this first version, then, Sheffield was supposed to be a contemporary of Craven. Juliana expanded on Iden's account in the same year:

In looking around for data concerning 'old Joe' we found his initials to be J. W. Sheffield and that he came to this country about 1765 directly from Staffordshire, England. We then found that Joe was the abbreviation for Josiah and we believe the W was for Wedgewood, Josiah Wedgewood Sheffield! In the shuffle the Wedgewood had been lost, but the spirit of the great Josiah has persisted in his descendants and Charles Teague, one of the potters at the Jugtown Pottery gets his heritage of old Joe through his forebears and Charles today is the first of the young men to enter the pottery profession seriously and with dignity.[48]

Because Juliana was herself a contributor to the Brown Collection, it seems a little odd that she herself did not submit the full song.

There is, however, enough mention of "Old Shuffle" in the newspaper accounts and in the Busbees' own writings, to reconstruct his evolution. He was first mentioned in the 1927 *News and Observer* article by Susan Iden:

In the section of Moore, Randolph, Montgomery and Chatham, near where the four counties join, Mr. Busbee found himself in a community of potters whose ancestry extends back to Revolutionary days, to a potter by the name of Sheffield, called "Shuffle" by the natives, and to one Peter Craven, who came to North Carolina from Staffordshire, England, in 1750.[47]

Martha Jane Owen makes molded clay chickens with her daughter, Ada [right, arms crossed] and Maxi [left] in the yard of their home, ca. early 1920s. A number of women and children in the Seagrove community made these chicken-shaped salt and pepper shakers for the Busbees. The ten cents they earned for each chicken often contributed significantly to their families' income.

Once the Busbees had made the imaginative leap from "Joe" to "Josiah" to "Josiah Wedgewood," it became an established fact within the Jugtown canon.

When Sheffield next appeared in 1929, he had become the Busbees' contemporary. In an article for *The Ceramic Age*, Jacques reported:

My adventures with old Josh Sheffield (pronounced Shuffle) and his blind mare and buggy over a radius of 25 miles of where the Jugtown Pottery is now established, is a story in itself. We slept on corded bedsteads in log cabins, we ate the simple food that was offered with lordly hospitality, we rummaged in lofts and smokehouses and cellars for ware, and what could not be bought was sketched or photographed.[49]

Two examples of the traditional salt-glazed stoneware jugs made by potters in the North Carolina Piedmont. Jug [left] made by Nicholas Fox, ca. 1850, Chatham County. Collection of William W. Ivey. Jug [right] made at J. D. Craven Pottery, ca. 1870s, Moore County. Collection of Ray Wilkinson.

Finally, a slightly earlier version of the story in Juliana's 1937 article appeared in a typescript of a speech by Juliana dated May 1, 1936. In this penultimate version, she reported, "One old potter who claimed Staffordshire descent and whose name was Sheffield (pronounced Shuffle) was a mine of information."[50]

The trail of "Old Joe Shuffle" apparently ends here, but a suggestive manuscript by Jacques provides further food for thought. Titled "A Colonial Hangover," it contains a version of Jacques's arrival in 1917. "I had great difficulty in finding someone willing to drive me the fifteen miles to the nearest pottery," he reported. "Once there I found myself amongst my 'contemporary Revolutionary ancestors' as Horace Kephart calls our mountain folk." After a description of bargaining for the pottery being used by his host "Martha Jane" to prepare supper, Jacques described the evening activities: "The evening meal being in the past, Martha Jane spun yarn while old Peter entertained the suspicious stranger with his fiddle - with tunes and jigs that few of this generation have ever heard."[51] In the manuscript, the typewritten name "Martha Jane" was crossed out in places and "Sarah Jane" substituted. In other places, "Peter," likewise, was replaced with "Josiah."[52]

At this point, Josiah Wedgewood Sheffield, a putative contemporary/historical individual, begins to look suspiciously like a literary conflation with Peter Craven, a historical individual who may have been a potter. Josiah's transformation from an ancestral figure to a 1920s contemporary of the Busbees may be a further

commingling with the actual figures of W. Henry and Martha Jane Scott, who boarded Jacques during his first years in Moore County; or James H. and Martha Jane Owen, who made pottery for the Busbees before they built the Jugtown Pottery.[53]

Yellow vase [left] with cobalt slip decoration, an early example of the art wares made at C. R. Auman Pottery, ca. early 1920s, Randolph County, N.C. The Wilkinson Collection. "Rebekah Pitcher" in "Mirror Black" glaze, made at J. B. Cole Pottery, ca. 1928, Montgomery County, N.C. Collection of William W. Ivey.

If the Busbees felt comfortable shaping the historical record to this extent, it was probably because they assumed the artistic authority to render the present-day rural landscape in a manner consistent with their vision of the tradition. "We found the people & their ways as foreign as European peasants," Juliana reminisced.

The landscape - their activities - their looks were picturesque & marvellous. One day in June during the wheat harvest we were watching the men cutting wheat with an old fashion cradle - the women binding the wheat - the babies parked on a quilt under a shade tree - boys in faded blue overalls with the large water jug & a gourd dipper running back & forth to…the thirsty harvesters - I asked my husband once how he could keep from painting the scene. He said the Barbizon school had done it perfectly - there was nothing new to add.[54]

Salt-glazed stoneware vase with cobalt slip and incised decorations made by J. H. Owen, ca. 1917, Moore County, N.C. This is an early example of the art wares made by Owen, possibly for the Busbees. The Wilkinson Collection.

Taking the perspective of a landscape painting, the Busbees could acknowledge their own separation from the culture of the area, while claiming the authoritative interpretive frame.

Upon their arrival in Moore County, the Busbees saw a pottery tradition that was severely moribund, a victim of expanding cosmopolitan markets and the deathblow of prohibition to the stoneware jug industry. Subsequent scholars have verified the grave effects of these developments on the pottery industry of the area, but their research on the

historical development of the industry suggests that the Busbees held a somewhat exaggerated view of the potteries' imminent demise. "When we came to this county those long years ago - there were only two or three old potters at work," reported Juliana, citing Rufus Owen, J. H. Owen, and Paschal Marable.[55] Yet according to Charles Zug, as the pottery industry of the region matured during the nineteenth century, a journeyman system of pottery making developed. This, together with the longstanding cultural pattern among the potters of moving between pottery, farming, and other occupations like sawmilling, blacksmithing, and woodworking, meant that there were many more active potters in the area than the Busbees perceived.[56]

There is little doubt that the developments noted by the Busbees were a deathblow for utilitarian wares, but from the perspective of the potters themselves, the Busbees' report of their death was certainly exaggerated. In turn, as these local potters seized opportunities afforded by an expanding market for decorative pottery, the Busbees downplayed their traditional authority: "The Auman pottery is run by Charlie Auman who is an expert saw mill man," sniffed Juliana in 1927. In the case of Jacon B. Cole, who established the very successful J. B. Cole Pottery around 1923, Juliana admitted that he "had been a potter years ago—had even worked with the German potters of Catawba, but had abandoned his wheel for saw milling until five or six years ago."[57] For the Busbees, the true potter was a practicing craftsman with an unbroken lineage: "Jugtown ware is the only surviving folkcraft pottery in the United States—'folkcraft' because it is an expression of a people through the urge of necessity. Its pedigree is unbroken since 1750," they declared on the menu card that graced the tables in Juliana's Greenwich Village tearoom.[58]

By their own account, the Busbees' intention apparently had been to organize a cottage industry among the remaining working potters still producing the utilitarian wares that had the essential primitive quality prized by the modernists. According to Ben Owen, who would become the main Jugtown potter, Henry Chrisco, Rufus Owen, James H. Owen, and J. W. Teague all turned wares that Jacques shipped to the tearoom Juliana established in Greenwich Village.[59] Among these, it appears that James H. Owen became the main potter supplying the Busbees during the period between 1917 and 1922. According to the Busbees, the experiment of moving pottery through a cottage industry was unsuccessful for several reasons. In the first place, the production system that was part of the potters' traditional culture was not conducive to the Busbees' vision: "It was difficult to find a man who would undertake to fill orders, even at what to him was a high price," reported Jacques. "After finding him, he proved so temperamental and filled orders so spasmodically that it became increasingly difficult to maintain a selling outlet in New York."[60]

The more serious problem from the Busbees' perspective was the inability of the potters to create a product that met with their artistic approval: "Here arose a further difficulty—to get the three or four old potters in this section who had stuck to their wheels . . . to produce pottery with sufficient finish and color to make it generally saleable. After five years of effort with these hard-baked old men, we realized that just so much time had been wasted."[61] One might ask how this could have happened when the Busbees had initially embraced the aesthetic integrity of these potters' utilitarian ware. The problem seems to have become intense once the translation of oriental forms instigated by Jacques had begun. "Old potters are hard baked," concluded Jacques. "Young potters are more plastic and can assimilate art training that is the absolute essential for any craft with more than a parochial interest."[62] The solution came with the building of the Busbees' own pottery shop around 1921 or 1922, where Jacques could create an environment modelled on his own notion of a traditional workshop; and with the hiring of teenagers Charlie Teague and Ben Owen.[63]

The conclusion one is led to from the Busbees' account is that the older potters were resistant to the artistic translations introduced by Jacques. "My husband found the old potter hard baked & difficult to inject into any art hyperdermic," claimed Juliana. "Then realizing that only youth is elastic & pliable, he began to search for young material."[64] From the potters' perspective, certainly in the case of James H. Owen, it may have appeared differently. According to his son, Melvin, J. H. Owen had decorated his salt-glazed ware with cobalt slip before meeting Busbee, and was quite open to the formal innovations Busbee introduced. The variety of oriental-influenced pieces turned by J. H. Owen that survive, some of them without the Jugtown stamp, seem to attest to this. By Melvin's account, J. H. happily continued to supply pottery to the Busbees for four or five months after they had built their own shop, up until his death in 1923: "He never had the privilege to work for them because he died the year they moved down there."[65] A statement by Jacques in Susan Iden's relatively early account also gives a different picture:

White glaze stoneware "Dogwood Vase" made by Ben Owen at Jugtown Pottery, ca. 1950. This vase was one of several translations of oriental forms developed by Jacques Busbee and Ben Owen. Collection of Pamela and Vernon Owens.

With the revival of interest in pottery, they went crazy and tried to copy every cheap, atrocious ten-cent store shape that they saw. When I would start them to work on a piece with instructions to 'turn a plank' or two all of the same shape, I would return to find that they had followed their own fancy and drifted away from the original design so far that there was no resemblance between the first and last pieces turned.

When I questioned one potter as to where he got such horrible shapes, he explained:

"Why I taken a Sears-Roebuck catalog and just plunked it out from the kivver." [66]

It was apparently not resistance to innovation that caused friction between the Busbees and the older generation, but the refusal of the older potters to render artistic authority to a cultural outsider.

The translation of oriental forms in Jugtown pottery was the culmination of what has been justly called "The Busbee Vision."[67] As Charles Zug has observed: "In retrospect Jacques Busbee's decision appears eminently correct. Recognizing the economic necessity of diversification, he focused on the wares of the Han, T'ang, and Sung Dynasties, which are best noted for their powerful forms, monochromatic glazes, and lack of elaborate surface decoration. These very general qualities also applied to the existing folk tradition in North Carolina, and thus young men like Ben Owen were able to comprehend the oriental models that Busbee presented to them."[68] The new direction was the true artistic triumph of Jacques's lifetime. In a letter he wrote from Jugtown to Juliana in New York sometime before 1922, the excitement of his insight is palpable:

I made a wonderful discovery to-day… Perhaps everyone else knows it already, but I saw it for myself. As the potter turns, the clay assumes various forms as he applies the various processes of opening out, pulling up, spreading, or narrowing the opening, et cetera. You cannot understand entirely unless you see the thing done, but as he turns, almost all of the shapes of antique Chinese pottery flicker before you in the technique of hand turning. What I mean is that Chinese and Japanese shapes are structural in the sense that they are the forms almost automatically developed by the technique employed. [69]

The ultimate artistic success of Jugtown derived from the internal consistency of this vision, and that consistency depended upon the Busbees' unswerving conception of the nature of tradition. Because they were an authentic expression of primitive art, the universalities expressed in ancient oriental ceramics were encoded in North Carolina pottery, and had only to be recovered. Here, where the older potters' hands faltered, Jacques's eyes saw the true translation.

It took the hands of young Charlie Teague and Ben Owen to bring the vision to formal life. The working collaboration between these individuals from divergent backgrounds is a matter for wonder. Here again, the participants' perspectives were probably quite different. On the Busbees' side, the creation of

Charlie Teague (above) and Ben Owen (left) turning pottery at Jugtown, ca. 1920s.

Jugtown pottery was a result of their own artistic vision, and the personnel who produced it were the skilled craftsmen working under their direction in their atelier. In the earlier accounts, Owen and Teague were simply "'Charlie' and 'Ben'" or "Two of the 'Jugtown Boys'".[70] In their own writings, the Busbees praised the abilities of the two, but within a somewhat paternalistic frame. Juliana wrote in 1927:

> It is through Charles Teague and Benjamin Wade Owen, their adaptable minds and magic fingers, their inheritance of reliability and steadfastness, that other young men will see the advantage of going into the profession seriously… The spirit of loyalty and of service is strongly developed in these two young men… The outstanding quality of these young men is their unswerving loyalty to the Jugtown Pottery in their work—their faithfulness of duty, their open minds and their great ability as artist craftsmen. Under the instruction of Jacques Busbee they are learning the fundamentals of all the plastic arts— sense of beauty in line and proportion.[7]

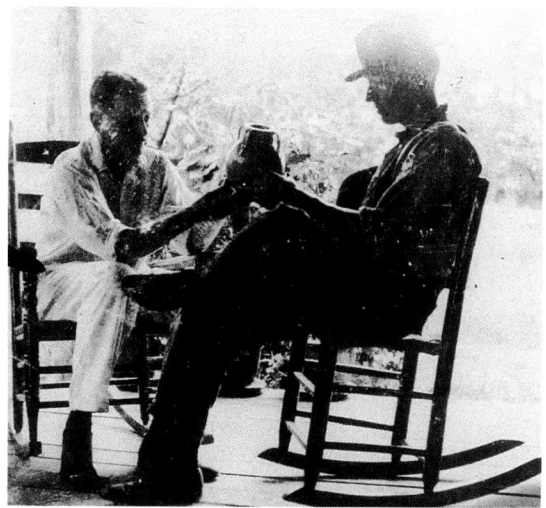

Ben Owen [left] and Juliana Busbee [right] pose at a table set with Jugtown pottery as part of a 1935 exhibit of gardens in Georgetown, Washington, D.C. This photograph, found in a newspaper clipping in the Country Roads' scrapbook, originally was taken by an unidentified staff photographer for the *Washington Herald* newspaper.

That quality of loyalty was not insignificant to the Busbees, who decried the fate of C. P. Ryman, who "attempted to reproduce the Wedgwood glazes & decoration" at his Skyland Pottery near Asheville: "He worked for several years until the man who worked for him thought he had learned all his secrets."[72] That potter, Walter B. Stephens, would become well known for his Pisgah Forest Pottery, while Ryman went out of business.

The relationship between the Busbees and the young potters would change over time, however. In the early accounts of the Pottery, it is Jacques who is identified as the "master potter," a title that may have derived from the Busbees' own presentation of their pottery as a craftsmen's workshop.[73] In the early hierarchy, Charlie Teague was ascendent, since the Busbees consistently emphasized his "ancestry dating back to Peter Craven of Staffordshire."[74] "Charles Teague, master potter, is a worthy son of his father and he is the first of the younger generation to adopt pottery as a serious, lucrative, dignified profession," noted Juliana in this same 1927 article that praised this young potter's loyalty.[75] At a celebratory barbeque staged at Jugtown in 1925 to publicize the inclusion of Jugtown pottery at the Southern Exposition in New York's Grand Central Palace, Charlie Teague was given central stage, according to the newspaper account.[76] But the Busbees became dissatisfied with Teague's working

habits over time, and after ten years eventually let him go.[77] By 1927, Juliana was also referring to Ben Owen as "Benjamin Wade Owen, master potter… from a long line of potters."[78] Ben Owen's travels with Jacques to visit museums in New York, Boston, Washington, and New Orleans, and with Juliana to demonstrate turning at garden parties and women's club meetings, clearly elevated his stature as a participant in the process.

Jacques Busbee [left] and Ben Owen [right] examine the form of a "Lily Jar" on the porch at Jugtown, ca. 1930.

Charlie Teague (left, kneeling), Jacques Busbee (center), and an unidentified man (right) in the yard at Jugtown, ca. 1920s.

But Ben Owen's public appearances soon began to establish him in the public mind as the potter of Jugtown. During the controversial period when John Maré acquired Jugtown in the 1950s, after Ben had left to begin his own Old Plank Road Pottery, the Jugtown loyalists declared, "the one man best qualified to carry on the designs and glazes perfected there is now turning them out under his own name, Ben Owen."[80] Once established at Old Plank Road, the place of "Ben Owen, Master Potter" became enshrined, and Ben Owen finally received the adulation that had earlier been the Busbees'.

On their side of the relationship with the Busbees, both Charlie Teague and Ben Owen clearly never conformed with the view that they were merely conduits for a larger artistic vision. At the 1925 Jugtown barbecue attended by politicians and crafts enthusiasts from all parts of North Carolina, Charlie Teague emphatically broke from this frame. According to reporter Clara Trenckmann, following a series of speeches by visiting dignitaries,

> . . . young Charlie Teague, a direct descendant
> of old Peter Craven, the leader of the original group
> in 1750, told Jacques Busbee, who was in charge
> of the affair, that he too wanted to make a speech.
> With a right good grace he spoke. In closing, he
> said: "I believe that my son is going to be the
> greatest potter that ever lived."[81]

For the Busbees, the hierarchical relationship between themselves and the local potters under their employ softened over time, but probably never entirely disappeared. Where Juliana referred to Charlie Teague and Ben Owen as master potters, it was in the framework of a studio system in which they were the craftsmen and Jacques was the artist. For Ben Owen, however, the rising stature of his position ultimately would not be circumscribed by the Busbees' own sense of his role. His standing among this growing circle of Jugtown aficionados would have its own life. As this process took place, the collectors and friends of Jugtown likewise elevated the term "Master Potter" from the rank of accomplished craftsmen, as used by the Busbees, to a term for artistic mastery.

At first, outsiders' perceptions matched the Busbees'. An early paeon indicates Teague's and Owen's initial status as viewed by a middle-class outsider:

> Jacques Busbee in the Carolina hills
> Is potter as the early settlers were.
> A lazy one-eyed mule goes round and round
> In endless circles to prepare his clay;
> Charlie and Ben, both native to the wheel,
> Have turned the lumps of clay for many years
> And fashioned vessels as Jacques taught them to.
> He says that he 'Svengalies' lovely forms
> From them, who only glimpse what beauty is.[79]

After Ben Owen had established his Old Plank Road Pottery, he finally gave his own version of the story in a brochure he created on the model of the earlier Jugtown pamphlets:

The front porch of the Busbees' cabin with several baskets, a stoneware jar, and pine branches arranged by Juliana to convey a sense of the rustic and the oriental aesthetics adopted by the Busbees.

Bob Owens passes a Korean bowl to Juliana Busbee for her to inspect while John Maré and Melvin Owens look on, ca. 1959.

While a young man, Mr. Owen became associated with Jacques Busbee, an artist. Together they visited the art schools and museums of New York, Washington, and New Orleans and selected designs which could be perfected with the media and methods that Mr. Owen knew.

As a result of this study they developed the world famous "Jugtown Ware," and began to fashion many interpretations of decorative and functional ware from the old Chinese, Korean, and Persian masters.[82]

"That Jugtown was a venture and expression of Mr. and Mrs. Busbee and myself is a fact," he declared elsewhere.[83] From the perspective of the potters, they were full collaborators in the creation of Jugtown and its pottery. And rightly so, for the potters' knowledge and skills acquired through their cultural upbringing contributed at least as much as the Busbees' artistic sensibility to the synthesis that was Jugtown. Where the Busbees decried the enthusiastic experimentation by area potteries with new glazes and forms, that creative, problem-solving impulse was an essential element of the very tradition they claimed to grasp; and it was this impulse Ben Owen actively brought to the process of creating the oriental translations with Jacques. In retrospect, the fairest and most accurate evaluation of Jugtown's history in the life of Moore County must view the contribution of local ideas and aesthetics as an active force, not merely a resource that the Busbees mined.

There remains, however, the "Jugtown Tradition" as a cultural phenomenon in and of itself. That creation did not take place in the interaction between the Busbees and Moore County potters, but in the Busbees' relationship to their own cultural world. First in Juliana's New York tearoom,

and then in their compound at Jugtown, the Busbees created a dramatic frame in which cosmopolitan consumers could encounter an idealized rendering of their own past. As an artistic creation, this was in large part Juliana's share in the collaboration. "I believed if I could properly magnetize the shop, get the right people together, give the same thing to the place that one gives a home - that people would come," she remarked of the tearoom.[84] In a setting that she managed as a literary salon, patrons encountered "a simple country store— serving plain N.C. food—on N.C. tables—with table cloths of N.C. gingham and on N.C. pottery plates & dishes."[85] It was a studied composition, just as the Busbees' handhewn log home in Moore County was a consciously contrived environment from the beginning. A reporter's 1924 account of the Jugtown Pottery nicely captures the effect:

. . . we pulled up before a charming log cabin built on simple lines so like—and yet so utterly unlike— anything seen in the entire countryside. Floating through

Ben Owen turning pottery at his Old Plank Road Pottery, ca. early 1970s.

Nancy Sweezy and Vernon Owens examine a piece of pottery after it has been fired in the kiln at Jugtown, ca. early 1970s.

*the intense summer heat were the strains of
Chaliapin's Volga Boat Song and on the long porch
across the front of the Jugtown cabin were bright
orange flower pots filled with velvety purple petunias,
and in a tall floor jar by the door was a branch of
pine—the whole thing so native and yet so strangely
Japonesque—that it took my breath.*[86]

At Jugtown, the charmed circle who gained admittance to the Busbees' world found a powerful and satisfying solution to the tension between progressivism and romanticism with which the Busbees had earlier struggled. This synthetic creation was no less culturally valid than the lifeways of the potter families in Moore County. It emerged from the experiences of urban North Carolinians, and generated a network of enduring associations. Its strength can be measured by the vehemence with which the disposition of Jugtown in the last years of Juliana's life was contested.[87] With the departure of Ben Owen, the source of "The Jugtown Tradition"—as it was embodied in the pottery— departed Jugtown, but continued under Ben Owen's hands at his own pottery. What was lost to Jugtown, the place, was gained in the authority that was due to Ben Owen, the potter.

For the circle of Jugtown aficionados the Maré period was indeed the end of Jugtown. For Vernon and Bobby Owens, the young sons of Melvin Owens, it was a difficult beginning. During the late 1950s and 1960s, the Owens brothers struggled to keep Jugtown going—Vernon turning while Bobby prepared the clay and glazes. Contracted by John

Maré to continue turning Jugtown pottery as it had been produced during the Busbee/Ben Owen years, Vernon Owens struggled between the formal constraints placed upon him by "The Jugtown Tradition," and the methods of pottery production he knew from his own family experience. When Maré died in 1962, Vernon and Bobby continued to lease the Pottery from his estate. Freed from the requirement that he copy the Jugtown forms under Maré's direction, Vernon Owens began to modify his pottery forms while attempting to remain in the Jugtown idiom.

While Vernon Owens was searching for his own solution to this problem, a new era at Jugtown began abruptly one afternoon in 1968 with the arrival of Nancy Sweezy from Cambridge, Massachusetts. A studio potter herself, Nancy had been a founding member of Country Roads, a venture to market Appalachian crafts in the urban Northeast. Visiting Jugtown at the suggestion of fellow Country Roads founder, Ralph Rinzler, Sweezy was powerfully seized by the place. "It was something like a conversion experience," she remembers. "Jugtown obviously played on some need in me."[88] Within a few months, Country Roads had purchased the pottery from Maré's estate, retaining Vernon and Bobby Owens as the working pot- ters, and Sweezy had instituted an apprenticeship program to train young potters in the Jugtown tradition. "Jugtown is one of the last traditional potteries in the entire coun- try," she told a newspaper reporter at the time. "We want to preserve this atmosphere and technique."[89]

potters. The artistic collaboration between Nancy Sweezy and Vernon Owens was no less complex, but from the very beginning it was one in which each recognized the active role the other would play. Sweezy envisioned her role from the perspective of a conservationist: "What I'm trying to do… is to keep the tradition, keep the historical aspect in a sense intact, but make it a viable operation for today," she told a reporter in 1970.[91] Yet the intention was never to preserve the pottery as a static monument. Abandoning the dangerous lead glazes of the Busbee era, Sweezy expanded the technical range of pottery produced at Jugtown to include safer, low-fired, fritted glazes, as well as higher-fired glazes and clay bodies. As the collaboration proceeded, Sweezy and Owens created a new vocabulary of Jugtown form with its own internal aesthetic consistency. The result was a new Jugtown pottery with an organic relation to the old.

"Neck Vase" [left] and low wide vase [right] are "Black Ankle" glaze stoneware made by Vernon Owens at Jugtown during the Country Roads period of ownership. Charles Moore developed the "Black Ankle" glaze in the early 1960s at Jugtown. "Neck Vase" from the collection of William W. Ivey. Low wide vase from the collection of Anne and Allen Bloom.

As Sweezy herself acknowledges, her own background, motives, and involvement with modern Jugtown hold a number of suggestive parallels with the Busbees' venture. Like the Busbees, Sweezy was a cultural outsider who began with an interest in bringing authentic traditional craft to a larger urban market. Like the Busbees, she entered a collaborative relationship with a local potter holding a different set of cultural assumptions. Like the Busbees, Sweezy saw in traditional pottery a form of modern redemption: "An awareness of folk art is an awareness of the roots of our social history, a link to our heritage," she declared in a pamphlet modelled on the Busbees' earlier ones. She continued,

> The individual craftsman must not only be a highly skilled technician but he must express a concept—his way of looking at life—through his hands. This expression contains the culture of his forebears, his own environment, and his own personality. Handwork must be sought, supported, and cherished because its life quality can balance the cold precision of the machine age.[90]

Where the Busbees had claimed the right to define the internal logic of the local pottery tradition, Sweezy entered Jugtown with a deep respect for the authority of the working

Pam Owens turning pottery at Jugtown, 1993.

"In a sense, I was helping people down here through a period of transition," Sweezy reflects today.[92] Upon her return to Boston in 1983, Country Roads sold the pottery to Vernon and Pam Owens. The couple continues to run Jugtown today. Pam, who began her own career as a working potter in the Country Roads apprenticeship program, is an accomplished turner in her own right, and is largely responsible for the development of new glazes at Jugtown today.

Another thread of the Jugtown tradition runs through Ben Owen's grandson, Ben Owen III, who began his career as a potter at the age of nine under the tutelage of his grandfather, by that time too crippled with arthritis to continue turning pottery. Beginning within the canon of form established by Ben Owen and Jacques Busbee, Ben III made a conscious decision to seek formal academic training in ceramics at East Carolina University. Today, he is the master potter in the shop that his grandfather built after leaving Jugtown, and is widely acknowledged as the heir to his grandfather's legacy.

Viewing the Moore County landscape today, one encounters an astonishing variety of active potteries—sixty-three at last count. By no means are these the direct descendants of the Busbees' Jugtown. They are, however, part of the complex matrix of tradition and innovation that found one expression at Jugtown, and emerged in other forms at the family potteries of the Coles, Teagues, Chriscos, and others. In the direct lineage of Jugtown—leading in one direction to Vernon and Pam Owens, and to Ben Owen in another—there is much to ruminate upon over the nature of tradition.

As a mature potter, Vernon Owens is highly regarded for the new forms he has developed that possess an internal consistency and grace equal to anything the Busbee vision created, while the glazes like "Claire de Lune" developed by Pam Owens exactly complimented the forms. Ironically, at the same time, the Jugtown Pottery of Vernon and Pam Owens is probably more firmly rooted in the working methods of the older family potters than Jugtown was during the Busbee era. In this regard, the vernacular tradition has reasserted itself in a modern realization that achieves all of the qualities the Busbees themselves were seeking. Ben Owen III, in his own evolution, has consciously built a career within the classic tradition of the artist that fueled the Busbees, purposely moving from the vernacular tradition to a cosmopolitan relationship with contemporary studio ceramics. In this direction local knowledge has gained control of artistic authority. Both directions are eminently satisfying and considerable accomplishments.

Taken as a whole, the Jugtown story is larger than any of its individual participants. Refracted and reformed, it cannot be advanced as an example of unbroken tradition as the Busbees asserted. The story nonetheless testifies to the vision they embraced, and which ultimately was greater than them. Jugtown is a powerful argument for the strength of cultural connections in the matrix of human creativity.

Some of the pottery signs that direct visitors to the more than 60 potteries in the region around Seagrove, N.C.

"Dragon Vase" with two dragon's head motifs attached at the shoulder with "Claire de lune" glaze, by Vernon Owens, 1993. During the Busbees' operation of Jugtown this form was known as a "Dogwood Vase." Collection of Pamela and Vernon Owens.

"Melon jar" with "Timaku" glaze made by Ben Owen III at Ben Owen Pottery, 1993. Collection of Ben Owen III.

Sugar jar (right) with bands of colored slip made by David Farrell at Westmoore Pottery, 1994. Though both David and Mary Farrell were apprentices at Jugtown, they have chosen to model their pottery after the wares produced by the Moravian potters working in the 18th and 19th century around Winston-Salem, North Carolina. This piece was modelled after a Moravian sugar jar in the collection of the Metropolitan Museum of Art pictured on a postcard found in the scrapbook of Juliana Busbee. Collection of David and Mary Farrell, Westmoore Pottery.

1 David Whisnant, *All That Is Native and Fine: The Politics of Culture in an American Region* (Chapel Hill: University of North Carolina Press, 1983), 13-14.

2 Jean Crawford has written the fullest and most balanced account to date, in *Jugtown Pottery: History and Design* (Winston-Salem, N.C.: John F. Blair, 1964). Crawford's purpose, however, was not to examine the Busbees' motives and intentions in relationship to the existing vernacular tradition.

3 William S. Powell, ed., *Dictionary of North Carolina Biography* 1 (Chapel Hill: University of North Carolina Press, 1979): 289; David B. Dearinger, Associate Curator of Painting and Sculpture and Archivist, National Academy of Design, New York, NY, to Jill Severn, 12 July 1993.

4 Crawford, *Jugtown Pottery: History and Design*, 11.

5 David B. Dearinger to Jill Severn, 12 July 1993; Lawrence Campbell, The Art Students' League of New York, to Jill Severn, 17 June 1993.

6 Mrs. Jacques Busbee, "Pottery in N.C.," Letter to the Editor, *The News and Observer*, 21 July 1929.

7 Juliana R. Busbee, "The Jugtown Pottery," TS, Mrs. Jacques Busbee Collection, North Carolina Department of Archives and History. Apparently copied from a handwritten ms. October 1940 and published in *Fashion Digest*, Winter 1941.

8 Jacques Busbee to Walter Clark, 5 September 1906, Walter Clark Papers, North Carolina Department of Archives and History.

9 Crawford, *Jugtown Pottery: History and Design*, 11.

10 "Busbes' Fine Pictures: Lecture on the Lost Roanoke Colony Greatly Enjoyed—A Talented Artist," *Hickory* [newspaper?], 22 April 1911. Found in a scrapbook kept at Jugtown over the years of its operation, now in the possession of Country Roads, Incorporated.

11 "Busbee Home Will Go Soon: Well Known Landmark and Relic of Old Raleigh to Be Torn Down," *The News and Observer*, 12 October 1914.

12 Undated newspaper fragment found among the Busbees' possessions at Jugtown by Nancy Sweezy.

13 The collection was published many years later by Duke University Press as *The Frank C. Brown Collection of North Carolina Folklore in Seven Volumes*, Newman Ivey White, general ed. (Durham, N.C.: Duke University Press, 1952).

14 Juliana R. Busbee to Frank C. Brown, 22 January 1915, *The Frank C. Brown Collection of North Carolina Folklore* 3, eds. Henry M. Belden and Arthur Palmer Hudson (Durham, N.C.: Duke University Press, 1952), 576-78.

15 She appears as "Miss Juliana Royster" in the Yearbook of the Raleigh Woman's Club for 1908.

16 Powell, *Dictionary of North Carolina Biography*, 1: 289.

17 Juliana Busbee to Woodrow Pruett, n.d., quoted in Crawford, *Jugtown Pottery: History and Design*, 36.

18 Juliana Busbee, untitled MS, n.d., Juliana Busbee Collection, Special Collections, University of North Carolina, Greensboro.

19 The Kirmess Kronikle, 2 February 1914, *Gertrude Weil Papers*, North Carolina Department of Archives and History.

20 Juliana Busbee, untitled MS, n.d., Juliana Busbee Collection.

21 Crawford, *Jugtown Pottery: History and Design*, 11.

22 Juliana Busbee, untitled MS, n.d., Juliana Busbee Collection.

23 Brochure for the Art Department of the State Federation of Women's Clubs, ca. 1915. Found in a scrapbook kept at Jugtown over the years of its operation, now owned by Country Roads, Incorporated.

24 Juliana Busbee, untitled MS, n.d., Juliana Busbee Collection.

25 Ibid.

26 Ibid.

27 Mrs. Jacques Busbee, "North Carolina Pottery and Pine Needle Baskets," *Everywoman's Magazine* 1, no. 1 (October 1916): 9.

28 Ibid.

29 Mildred Harrington, "Interesting People: The Master Potter of Jugtown," *The American Magazine* CIII, no. 6 (June 1927): 74.

30 Mrs. Jacques Busbee, "Pottery in N.C."

31 Letter from Juliana Busbee, 9 November 1941, quoted in "The Craft Potters of North Carolina: Busbee, Hilton, and Stephen, The Influence of Oscar Louis Bachelder," *The Bulletin of the American Ceramic Society* 21, no. 6 (15 June 1942): 80-87.

32 Juliana Busbee, "Art hath an enemy called ignorance," MS, ca. 1939, Juliana Busbee Collection, Special Collections, University of North Carolina, Greensboro.

33 Juliana Busbee, untitled MS, n.d., Juliana Busbee Collection. Juliana's Greenwich Village tearoom may well have begun as some type of formal association with the North Carolina Federation of Women's Clubs. Gretchen M. Bayne, who may have been the Mrs. T. L. Bayne active in promoting handweaving in North Carolina, is listed with Juliana at the Village Store in *Trow's General Directory of the Burroughs of Manhattan and Bronx, City of New York*, 1918-19 (New York: Trow Directory, Printing and Bookbinding Co.).

34 "A Fine Record," newspaper fragment located in scrapbook kept at Jugtown Pottery which is now owned by Country Roads, Incorporated. [This probably came from either the *Raleigh Times* newspaper or *The News and Observer*, ca. 1917 or 1918.]

35 Susan Iden, "Jacques Busbee Sets Many Potters' Wheels Turning Again in the State," *The News and Observer*, 1927.

36 Juliana Busbee, "The Discovery of Folk Pottery," MS, n.d., Mrs. Jacques Busbee Collection, North Carolina Department of Archives and History.

37 Juliana R. Busbee, "The Jugtown Pottery."

38 See Beatrix T. Rumford, "Uncommon Art of the Common

People: A Review of Trends in the Collecting and Exhibiting of American Folk Art," in Ian M. G. Quimby and Scott T. Swank, eds., *Perspectives on American Folk Art* (New York: W. W. Norton & Company, 1980), 13-53.

[39] Mrs. Jacques Busbee, Letter to the Editor, *The News and Observer*, 21 July 1929.

[40] Juliana R. Busbee, "The Jugtown Pottery."

[41] Jacques Busbee, "A Colonial Hangover," TS, ca. late 1920s, Juliana Busbee Collection, Special Collections, University of North Carolina, Greensboro. In the manuscript, the last sentence is crossed out.

[42] The claim first appears in Iden, "Jacques Busbee Sets Many Potters' Wheels Turning Again in the State."

[43] Charles G. Zug III, *Turners and Burners: The Folk Potters of North Carolina* (Chapel Hill: University of North Carolina Press, 1986), 42-43.

[44] Juliana R. Busbee, "Jugtown Pottery—A New Way for Old Jugs," *Bulletin of the American Ceramic Society—Communications* XVI, no. 10 (October 1937): 415-18. The Busbees reprinted the article as a pamphlet entitled "A New Way For Old Jugs," which was apparently distributed at the Pottery. Juliana R. Busbee, "A New Way for Old Jugs," reprint from *Bulletin of the American Ceramic Society* (October, 1937) [c. 1937]. It was reprinted again, with minor changes, as "The Genesis of Jugtown" not long after Jacques's death. Juliana R. Busbee, "The Genesis of Jugtown," reprint from *Bulletin of the American Ceramic Society* (October, 1937) [c. 1948]. Dating is based on internal evidence: "A New Way for Old Jugs" contains the sentence, "Remember that twenty years ago, when we began this adventure, this was a mauve world, and color had not been encouraged to brighten the corners." In "The Genesis of Jugtown," this is changed to "thirty-one years ago."

[45] Juliana R. Busbee, "Jugtown Pottery—A New Way For Old Jugs," 415.

[46] Crawford, *Jugtown Pottery: History and Design*, 17.

[47] Iden, "Jacques Busbee Sets Many Potters' Wheels Turning Again in the State."

[48] Juliana Busbee, "Age-Old Profession Now Flourishes in Sand Hills," *The News and Observer*, 5 June 1927.

[49] Jacques Busbee, "Jugtown Pottery: Its Origin and Development—An Intimate Touch of the Local Color That is Molded Into This Historic American Ware," *The Ceramic Age* (October 1929): 128.

[50] Juliana R. Busbee, TS, 1 May 1936, Juliana Busbee Collection, Special Collections, University of North Carolina, Greensboro.

[51] Jacques Busbee, "A Colonial Hangover."

[52] Portions of the manuscript are quoted in Ruth Kedzie Wood, "Jugtown, where they make Jugs," *The Mentor* (April 1928): 33-36.

[53] According to Vernon Owens, W. H. Scott was a musician and may have been a fiddler. In Jacques's manuscript, we are told that Peter/Josiah "is considered the best potter in the settlement, although I discovered later that he had an almost equal talent for

praying at meeting." In other places, the Busbees describe J. H. Owen as "a holy roller preacher." For example, in a manuscript that probably dates from the period of Jacques's death, Juliana writes: "When we came to this county those long years ago - there were only two or three old potters at work. One was the father of our present potter - who did crocks & churns & pickle jars - An old potter named Jim Owen who was a holy roller preacher & who did occasional crocks & churns - Then there was one named Paschal Marable." Juliana Busbee, "The Discovery of Folk Pottery," MS, n.d., Mrs. Jacques Busbee Collection, North Carolina Department of Archives and History. The Busbees' characterization of J. H. Owen as a "holy roller preacher" is disputed by James's son Melvin.

[54] Juliana Busbee, "The Discovery of Folk Pottery."

[55] Ibid.

[56] See Zug, *Turners and Burners*, 262-71.

[57] Juliana Busbee, "Age-Old Profession Now Flourishes in Sand Hills," 1, 7.

[58] "Native American Pottery for Decoration and Household Use," *New York Sunday Tribune*, 31 March 1924.

[59] Crawford, *Jugtown Pottery: History and Design*, 19.

[60] Mrs. Jacques Busbee, "Pottery in N.C."

[61] Jacques Busbee, "Jugtown Pottery: Its Origin and Development," 129.

[62] Mrs. Jacques Busbee, "Pottery in N.C."

[63] Crawford, *Jugtown Pottery: History and Design*, 21.

[64] Juliana Busbee, "The Jugtown Pottery."

[65] Melvin L. Owens, interview with author, Seagrove, N.C., 12 January 1994.

[66] Iden, "Jacques Busbee Sets Many Potters' Wheels Turning Again in the State."

[67] Gay Mahaffey Hertzman, *Jugtown Pottery: The Busbee Vision* (Raleigh, N.C.: North Carolina Museum of Art, 1984), exhibition catalog. The formal relationship of the Busbees' oriental translations to their Han, T'ang, Sung, and Middle Eastern originals is discussed at length by Mahaffey in her catalog essay.

[68] Zug, *Turners and Burners*, 393.

[69] Letter from Jacques Busbee to Juliana Busbee, quoted in Jessie Martin Breese, "Jugtown, N.C.," *Country Life* (October 1922): 64.

[70] Iden, "Jacques Busbee Sets Many Potters' Wheels Turning Again in the State;" Harold Essex, "Story of 'The Master Potter of Jugtown': He and Wife Revive Lost Art in N.C.," *Greensboro Daily Record*, 10 November 1928.

[71] Juliana Busbee, "Age-Old Profession Now Flourishes in Sand Hills."

[72] Juliana Busbee, untitled MS, ca. 1940, Juliana Busbee Collection, Special Collections, University of North Carolina, Greensboro.

73 See for example Mildred Harrington, "Interesting People: The Master Potter of Jugtown," *The American Magazine* (June 1927): 72-74; Essex, "Story of 'The Master Potter of Jugtown': He and Wife Revive Lost Art in N.C."; "Master Potter Makes Address: Jacques Busbee, Known in N.C., as Master Potter, Will Be In Suffolk for Talk Tonight," Suffolk, Virginia [Newspaper?], 6 December 1928.

74 Iden, "Jacques Busbee Sets Many Potters' Wheels Turning Again."

75 Juliana Busbee, "Age-Old Profession Now Flourishes in Sand Hills."

76 Clara Trenckmann, "Jugtown Potters Win Praise In Big New York Exposition," *The News and Observer*, 31 May 1925.

77 Crawford, *Jugtown Pottery: History and Design*, 24.

78 Juliana Busbee, "Age-Old Profession Now Flourishes in Sand Hills."

79 Albert V. Fowler, "Jugtown," *Aberdeen Pilot*, 13 March 1931. The remainder of Fowler's poem provides a further view of Busbee's artistic universe:

> He burns the hand-glazed clay in two brick kilns,
> Low built and long beneath a rough wood roof;
> One peers through red-gold sheets of flame to see
> The bowls and jars that glow with borrowed fire.
> In the small cabin made of mud and logs
> Jacques shows you many vases, ancient blue,
> Of early Persian and Chinese design.
> The Chinese potter is his chief delight;
> He thinks the potter in the reigns of Han
> Discerned and crystallized those perfect shapes
> That are the essence of the clay and wheel.
> Jacques knows the wet clay on the wheel so well
> That as it changes shape in Charlie's hands
> The unseen elements of form that called
> And tantilized the Chinese potter's mind
> Flicker before him between change and change.
> Something in the very working of the clay
> Appeals to Jacques and is his happiness—
> A harking back to the primeval man
> Who made clay vessels as Jacques makes them now;
> A bond of union with the racial strength
> That dances, sings and paints for pure delight;
> Deeps of emotion linking us with men
> Clothed in the mystery of ancient times.

80 Editorial, "Can Jugtown Go On?" *Winston-Salem Journal*, 28 August 1962.

81 Clara Trenckmann, "Jugtown Potters Win Praise In Big New York Exposition," *The News and Observer*, 31 May 1925.

82 "Ben W. Owen: Master Potter," pamphlet, ca. early 1960s.

83 Ben Owen, "Letter to the Editor," *Winston-Salem Journal*, 5 September 1962.

84 Juliana Busbee, untitled MS, 1931.

85 Crawford, *Jugtown Pottery: History and Design*, 26-27. The quote is from a manuscript attributed to Juliana.

86 Betty Graham, "Betty Graham Visits Jugtown," *The News and Observer*, 31 August 1924.

87 A full account of the struggle between Jugtown Incorporated and John Maré to gain control of the Pottery can be found in Crawford, *Jugtown Pottery: History and Design*, 39-55.

88 Nancy Sweezy, interview with author, Jacksonville, Fla., 18 October 1992 and Robbins, N.C., 8 December 1992.

89 Charles Heatherly, "Fabulous Jugtown: A New Era and New Owner for World-Famous Pottery," *Greensboro Daily News*, 24 November 1968.

90 Nancy Sweezy, "The Jugtown Story," pamphlet, n.d. Nancy Sweezy also is the author of *Raised in Clay: The Southern Pottery Tradition* (Washington, D.C.: Smithsonian Institution Press, 1984).

91 Eleanor Dare Kennedy, "She Cast Her Lot In Jugtown," *Greensboro Daily News*, 18 January 1970.

92 Nancy Sweezy, interview with author.

To the Editor

Jacques Busbee

Jacques Busbee, ca. 1890-1905.

The original handwritten draft of this text is part of the Juliana Royster Busbee Manuscript Collection assembled by Blackwell Robinson, Emeritus Professor of History at the University of North Carolina, Greensboro. Professor Robinson gave the Collection to the Walter Clinton Jackson Library at the University of North Carolina, Greensboro.

In the following transcription, an effort has been made to retain all original features of the handwritten text authored by Jacques Busbee, including misspellings, and idiosyncratic paragraphing, punctuation, and capitalization. Misspellings are followed by "[sic]" to indicate their status as part of the original text. Words that were not entirely legible in the original handwritten copy of Jacques Busbee's "Letter to the Editor" appear in brackets, as do words the catalog editors inserted to make sense of particular sentences.

To the Editor:

Dear Sir: The time has come to publish the true facts concerning the Jugtown Pottery about which many New York magazines and newspapers have written so much, and about which the state papers have mis-written so much with the notable exception of Mildred Harrington's articles.

"Jugtown Ware" is the growth of an interest extending over many years. The specimens in our collections of this folk craft pottery which we brought to New York, created such enthusiasm among the artists and ceramic experts who saw it, that we decided to make the attempt to put this unique product of our state on the world market. Up to this time the work of our Country Potters had only traveled in covered wagons. Yet we were without funds or backing for so large an enterprise except for our faith and enthusiasm.

The first requirement was to secure sufficient stock for a try-out in New York City. North Carolina is a very large state—the potters were scattered in groups over widely separated areas, and the question was where to go in the state for our stock.

Roughly speaking the potters fell into three groups—the Catawba County "Dutch" and the remnants of the Forsythe [sic] County Moravians: the potters around Asheville who were not native potters (with one exception) and the potters descended from the Staffordshire settlers in the section where Moore, Randolph, and Montgomery Counties join.¹

We decided on the last named section as the most interesting place to begin our operations, and our reasons were these: Early in the eighteenth century some potters from Staffordshire, England had settled in this section and their descendants [were] still making ware reminiscent of the old English shapes and glazes which connoeurs [sic] fight over in auction rooms.² These potters had remained uninfluenced by the outside world for over a hundred & fifty years and their work had a character and interest unique.

It was in May 1917 that we began our venture in the extreme North West corner of Moore County.

We found the country potters languishing, even more, they were moribund—and State prohibition laws of years standing were the cause. There was no longer any money to

be made in the production of jugs. Where fifty kilns once made a good living with orders from the distilleries a half dozen potters could now supply the country neighborhood with jugs for vinegar or sorghum syrup, with churns, crocks and butter jars, pitchers and stew pots. "Toy stuff" as the potters called table ware—the "dirt dishes" of the Civil War period—were not in demand, since white "chiney" was abundant and cheap. The price of ware had fallen to ten cents and lower, a gallon.

But "toy stuff" and "dirt dishes" of the Civil War period were patently the only types of pottery that would have a present day use or a wide appeal.

The potters who were still operating their shops in this Saffordshire [sic] section were all men past middle life. They farm on the side for a support, as there was little profit in ware making, even though the family did much of the work around the shop, and without pay. Even the wood for the kiln was cut on the potter's own [land]—as a rule and cost only the labor.—

The potters' sons, with generations of craftmanship [sic] in their hands, were straying off to saw mills or to cotton and furniture factories; in fact, to any job that offered a living wage.

Between the time of our first visits some eight or ten years before, and our return in 1917 there was woeful falling off in the quality as well as the output. The potter had lost faith in himself as well as in his market. He had lost his tradition and was feebly attempting to imitate factory made stuff of the ten cent store variety in the desparate [sic] hope of getting back his market.

It was difficult to find a man who would undertake to fill orders, even at what to him was a high price. After finding him, he proved so temperamental and filled orders so spasmodically that it became increasingly difficult to maintain a selling outlet in New York. Something else had to be done.

First the entire section was searched for old ware in order to reestablish [sic] the best local traditions. Some pieces found dated to within two generations of Peter Craven who was one of the original settlers.

Then young men in the line of descent were employed who were capable of art training—and then we built the Jugtown Pottery shop eight miles from Hemp in Moore County.

Old potters are hard baked—young potters are more plastic and can assimilate art training that is the absolute essential for any craft with more than a parochial interest.

The young men who work under Art direction at the Jugtown Shop are now producing pottery that is interesting the Art Collectors and the Museums all over the United States. Shipments of pottery from our kilns have gone to England, France, Hawaii & of course, all over the States and to Canada—New Zealand, Australia—Brazil.³

In the beginning a trade name was necessary, so we registered a trade mark (stamped on the bottom of all our output) that has mystified and misled the State in a way not intended. Formerly "Jugtown" was a local nickname for any section in the state where two or three potters were gathered together. It was not considered an honorific title. The Jugtown which achieved the distinction of a post office was in Catawba County among the "Dutch"—⁴

And so we took "Jugtown Ware" for a trade mark as a certain historical significance was implicit in the name itself.

North Carolina pottery is of no consequence in itself, without beauty. Being made of N.C. dirt adds nothing to its value unless it is embodied into the forms of Art. For as a matter of fact the whole of art *is* form. We call it form in pottery and sculpture: proportion in architecture: good drawing in paintings: feeling or soul in music: style in literature. Pottery without beauty of form cannot be made interesting by color glaze or decoration. The state may accept it from misplaced pride but the world never will.

Jugtown Pottery is now the pace maker for our community. The other potters have been stimulated into imitation, and though their attempts are crude, the effort is in the right direction and ultimately will bring results.[5] Already it has brought financial results, for the roadside potters have a tourist clientele as innocent of Art as the potters themselves.

It is enormously gratifying to know that the state has established within the past year, a department of ceramics at the A.& M. College. Technical knowledge is the necessary foundation on which the future artist potters must build.

Portrait painting in North Carolina is close akin to the Mortician, for Art that has no practical, present day use is as dead as its subjects. To train the younger men in a sense of beauty, form, fitness; to keep alive the most interesting folk craft tradition in the United States today, seemed to us a task undertaken for our state and worthy of any sacrifice involved.

[As] North Carolinians it seemed incumbent upon us to make some contribution to the state, as our forebears [sic] had done. Art applied to a community is no longer a selfish luxury but, as it seems to us, an effort closely parallelling [sic] patriotism.[6]

Jacques Busbee

[1] What appears to be the word "Wilkesboro" is written in the margin to the left of this paragraph.

[2] The corrected spelling "connoisseurs" is written lightly above "connoseurs."

[3] Written lightly below "Canada and New Zealand" are what appear to be the words "China—Korea or Japan."

[4] In parentheses following the word "Dutch" are what appear to be the words "lasted 18 months—star route."

[5] Above the word "crude" appears a question mark.

[6] A question mark is written lightly following the word "luxury."

Jugtown Pottery

Juliana Busbee

Juliana Busbee, ca. 1920s.

The following text is a transcription of a handwritten draft of an article Juliana Busbee authored in 1940 for Fashion Digest. *The draft exists as part of the Juliana Royster Busbee Manuscript Collection at the Walter Clinton Jackson Library at the University of North Carolina in Greensboro.*

All features of the handwritten text have been retained, including idiosyncracies in paragraphing, punctuation, and spelling. Misspellings are followed by "[sic]" to signal that these were part of the original text. All ampersands in this published text appeared as such in the handwritten version. Punctuation marks inserted by the editors for clarification are bracketed.

There are considerable differences between the transcription which follows and the article, "Jugtown Pottery," by Juliana Busbee, published in the Winter 1941 issue of Fashion Digest. *Since it is not clear whether Juliana Busbee or a* Fashion Digest *editor was responsible for the many changes in the organization and tone of the article, the catalog editors decided to reprint the version of the text which retains the flavor of an early draft.*

A typewritten transcription of another draft of this same article exists as part of the Mrs. Juliana Busbee Collection (P.C. 378) housed at the North Carolina Department of Cultural Resources' Division of Archives and History in Raleigh. Since it is not clear who created this typewritten transcription, the editors have chosen to reprint the version of the text which could be verified as having been authored by Juliana Busbee.

Fashion Digest
Oct 1940

It seems strange, doesn't it, to have one's whole life— and the lives of a whole community, turned upside down by a pie plate. And an empty one at that.

Although the dish was apparently empty the color was joyous, and to us it was filled with visions of what might be.

I found the plate at a county fair. Even though I lost my head, I found a fresh enthusiasm.

After all, isn't modern art just that: losing one's head? Haven't artists been using their intellects instead of their eye sight?

As I understand the modern trend of Art—it is the impulse to wipe the retina clean—thereby seeing with it instead of the brain. And refusing to be influenced by the art critics—seeing as instructed.

Fraternizing with the modern art Exponents of the new movement some twenty odd years ago that clarified in our minds our attitude toward the country crafts.[1] We came to see them as a modern Primitive expression. After we perceived that idea, life held nothing for us but to see the thing through in our own native state in our own way. So we hypnotized ourselves into believing that the Jugtown Pottery was the one thing in life to work with and for and through.

I had always loved the soft grey [sic] pickle jars and crocks and pitchers for flower arrangements—particularly for things from the fields and woods.

We believed that a little art direction to the country potter who made these things would bring a new industry to our state and rescue a craft that was fast disappearing.

At the time there were few Highways in North Carolina. It was long before the good roads era. The potters were far from the bad roads we had.

That foresaid revolutionary Pie Plate was found in a country store. It was not considered a work of art I assure you. It was difficult to learn where it had been made. The brilliant color was plainly in the clay.

We knew there were infinite possibilities in that clay— and in its Potter who made it. Had I been able to look down the years in that plate and foresee the hard work and sacrifices the development entailed, I would not even then have faltered in our undertaking.

We made every effort to shift the development of the craft to other shoulders. We had no idea we could do it[.] Artists in those days were not supposed to be practical—and the idea we had no precedent to recommend the venture.

At that time we were frightfully bored painting portraits no one liked, and landscapes that no one would buy. So we escaped to New York where we planned to spend a year. And we became violent converts to modern art. We knew the development of an American craft might well be launched at that time. It was during the World War. The lovely peasant things from Europe could not reach this market—and there was no native simple pottery on sale anywhere in this country.

Now that is how it all began.

When my husband came to this part of our state in the Pie Plate Quest, he had strange and unbelievable experiences. He was suspected of being a German spy, because one of our neighbors said "he seen a german onct & my husband out favored him." To this day we are foreigners to this little country world.

But Mr. Busbee did not mind these innumerable amusing hinderances [sic]. All he was interested in was finding the potters, and helping the decrepit craft to kick again.

You see, from the beginnings of English America there have been potters here. Cut off from the outside world through bad roads and poverty, they supplied themselves & their neighbors with all the necessities for living. Dishes to eat from—to cook in, for churns and pitchers and medicine jars—containers for all their needs. To say nothing of weaving cloth for their clothes, their beds—making their own shoes from home tanned hydes [sic]—their own baskets—their own black smithing—and farming besides.

Unfortunately for the potters, our state nobly experimented with prohibition. Those who made jugs for the whiskey distilleries were cut off from their source of livelihood[.] That blow came about 1908, I think. Then the potters abandoned their wheels & went to saw mills, factories—& pulpits.

That was the situation here when Jacques Busbee of Raleigh entered the picture.

We had made a valiant effort to arouse enthusiasm for what we thought a bright idea. But no one else could see eye to Pie Plate with us.

I suppose, however, that one is not dependent on the interest of others, if the fires of enthusiasm burns and blazes sufficiently. That fire has lighted our own way for twenty three years and shows no evidence of extinction.

We found if the craft was to survive we must pump the saline solution into the moribund potters.

To do that meant sharing the life and hardships of the people here.

Our geographical location at that time was remote due to impassable roads. Since the state has taken over the Highways, we are now accessible—to the determined.

We elected this isolated [little] to work with because of the clay that burned such a lovely color—

The place was delightfully different from any place we had ever known. We were kept constantly stimulated and tantalized. Had we been real students of English, of History, of Sociology, of Ethnology, we would have been even more thrilled. But even with our scant knowledge there was much to detect and trace. The obsolete English, the feudal customs, the pioneer habits and manners, gave the days delight, and made theatre of it all.[2]

My husband found the old potters hard baked and allergic to art, so to speak. For several years the work was without satisfying results. Then realizing that only youth is elastic and pliable, he began to search for young material. Descendants of the older men abounded. In a short time Jugtown Pottery was attracting attention from the country at large.

The name Jugtown was chosen because we thought the state's pottery was implicit in the name. In the early days, whenever a few potters were found, in derision, the section was termed Jugtown—because of course they all made Jugs for liquor. Although the name was forsworn, we thought it such a thorough discard we rescued it from the trash heap and registered it.

At first the old potters thought the name a huge joke. But when magazine articles came in quick succession, the name was claimed by every potter in the state—as was the Staffordshire ancestry of the men who worked here whose lineage was laborously [sic] & painstakingly traced.[3]

That claim to our trade name has caused endless confusion.[4] Now there are many potter shops—several of them capitalized with outside money & a tremendous out put of gay pottery is shown on every highway from Maine to Florida. All of it called "Carolina Pottery[.]"

The aim of my husband has been to keep the small out put of the Jugtown Pottery in character with its crude sur-roundings.[5] To hold the production to the same tempo of the pre Revolutionary potter. To keep the tradition of this settlement with only slight edited editions of those early utilitarian dishes. To use the same people, the same fabric, the same technique, unaltered since those 1740 days[.]

When other things are done, Mr. Busbee goes to the very early Chinese for form.[6] For he thinks the potters of the Han, the T'ang, the Sung Dynasties worked in much the same way of our back woods country potter.[7] He has tried

to teach beauty of form and line. And color in its relation to form. He believes that Primitiveness is a state of mind— not a Point in Time.

[1] The word "that" was written, but crossed out, between the words "ago" and "clarified."

[2] The word "Elizabethan" was crossed out before the word "obso-lete" in the handwritten text.

[3] "Jugtown" appeared crossed out before the word "men" in this sentence.

[4] The original sentence featured the word "register" before the word "trade," and ended with the phrase "and many people do not know that," both of which were crossed out.

[5] The phrase, "the Jugtown Pottery," initially appeared after "keep," but was crossed out.

[6] The following sentence appeared but was crossed out in the hand-written draft: "He has authority for every shape down here—noth-ing is improvised."

[7] Written in pencil after the word "potter" are the words "classic period."

Perspectives

The following statements were drawn from interviews with the individuals cited. Each was gracious enough to offer their own perspective on, and in some cases to reflect on their participation in, the history and significance of the Jugtown Pottery.

Jugtown, Where They Make Jugs

REMEMBERING THE FIRST POTTERS AT JUGTOWN

The Jugtown Christmas Tree, 1926

From left to right, front row: Hoover Reeder, Alta Reeder, Alton Needham, Lucy Reeder, unknown girl, Margaret Scott, William Reeder, William Scott, Ruby Reeder, unknown boy, James Scott, Parence Needham. Second row: Jason Reeder, Lula Reeder holding John Reeder, Myrtle Needham, Ola Brown, Lily Scott Needham, Catherine Needham (wearing bonnet), unknown woman, unknown boy. Third row: Claud Scott, Martha Jane Scott, Nora Needham, Ella Scott holding baby, Bertie Moore. Back row: James Needham, Abija Scott, John Needham (Santa Claus), Jacques Busbee, Clifford Moore, Dewey Brower or Joe Needham holding baby, Herbert Scott, Walter Ritter or Henry Moore, Charlie Teague, Ben Owen. This photograph was taken around Christmas time in 1926. Many of these people worked at Jugtown. Others at this gathering probably were from the Seagrove area. Photograph was probably taken by Juliana Busbee.

Charles G. Zug III

Charles G. Zug III, Professor of Folklore and English, University of North Carolina, Chapel Hill, North Carolina. He is the author of Turners and Burners: The Folk Potters of North Carolina.

If the Busbees hadn't existed, would there be anybody making pottery today? I think that's a very tantalizing question. I don't think anybody really knows the answer. I have a feeling that probably one or two of those potters could have kept going and somehow made the transition. I think the crucial period was probably the twenties. I think the Coles would have made it. That family had a lot of self-awareness, and of course J. B. Cole had his pottery in 1921 or 1922, the same time as Jugtown, and it did well. I think the Cole family and probably some of the others would have pulled it through. There would have been something, some thread would have been unbroken. Southern Pines and Pinehurst are sitting right down below them, and people were coming up in the late nineteenth century to see these potters. And that North-South Route 1 was like Interstate 95 today. I think it would have kept going. But these extraordinary oriental translations that the Busbees brought wouldn't have happened. Somehow they picked up on what was going on in the late nineteenth century and the early twentieth century arts and crafts movement, and brought it down and blended it down here, and it lasted longer here than it did anywhere else. It's still here.

Right about the same time the Busbees got there, around World War I, other artists in this country had gone out and begun collecting folk art. This was our primitive art, our medieval past. It was like collecting African art or the Japanese woodblocks that French artists were interested in. So collectors like the Rockefellers and the Fords got to collecting folk art along with modern art. And if you get people like that interested, that's got to have helped enormously.

This is going to be an odd comparison, but one of the things I've always felt about the Busbees was that they were a little bit like Joel Chandler Harris. They were both artistically inclined, but frustrated. Harris was also frustrated—he was a frustrated novelist. The Busbees took a folk art and restructured it and made it their own, just like Harris took folk tales and put them into that plantation framework with Uncle Remus and Daddy Jake. I don't mean this conde-scendingly, but I think this was their art: they didn't make the pottery, but they really shaped it.

Aside from it being art, I think for the Busbees it was a kind of nostalgic play-acting, indulging in the past. Obviously the way they lived down there was very different from the

way they lived in Raleigh or New York. But I think for them it was an experience that worked for them aesthetically and psychically. I think they enjoyed partly living in the past and they did it pretty well.

The Busbees had that ability to merchandise their things. Selling the pottery was probably the greatest thing they did. They brought new ideas into this old traditional world, and they brought new people in to learn about it and appreciate it. It was part of this spectacle that they put on, that's what I'd call it. They gave the people who came in there a genuine kind of tourist experience. What the people walked away with were souvenirs—very nice and authentic souvenirs. The Busbees were very good at orchestrating that, and there are people who come to Moore County even today looking for that experience. The Busbees helped to bridge that experience by arranging things for people. They got outsiders to experience this culture, but not make it too radical a shock.

Henry and Rebecca Cooper were like the Busbees. They came in and did the same thing with the North State Pottery in 1925. They wrote articles and had a little catalog about the Staffordshire origins of the pottery, too. This was part of the whole process of authenticating the pottery. They took the North State pottery to the Sesquicentennial in Philadelphia in 1926, like the Busbees had gone to New York. They took up a half of a log cabin, and they had something like a stage setting, very much like going to Mr. and Mrs. Busbee's house—a log house with hard pine flooring and slatback chairs and coverlet curtains. To sell that pot-tery to people you had to put it into this particular sort of setting to make it palatable and attractive. Otherwise I don't think it would have made much sense. Their expression went beyond the pots—it was a whole ambiance. Obviously Ben Owen couldn't have done that, or any of the Owenses or Cravens or Coles. They didn't understand these new people, but the Busbees and the Coopers knew this.

The old potters would open the kiln and put the pottery right out on the grass next to the kiln. That was as far as it ever went. Most old potters didn't even have a little shed to put it in. Eventually it would go into a wagon or truck and it would go off and be sold in a different neighborhood or hardware store. Just think of the difference between piling the pottery on the ground and putting it into a display shop, or putting it into your dining room or living room and selling it right out of your house.

I remember talking about Jugtown with an old journeyman potter named Jack Kiser a long time ago. He was working in the thirties and forties when all this was going on. He said they made a pitcher at A. R. Cole's that they sold for fifty cents. And he said Mr. Busbee sold the same pitcher for six dollars. Then he laughed. Jack Kiser was a first-rate joker, and he probably exaggerated, because I can't believe there'd be that much difference. But the point he made was that the Busbees had the skill to set the pottery up and sell the same thing for three or four times as much as the other potteries could get. The other potteries didn't know how to deal with these people the way the Busbees did.

The thing that makes Mr. Busbee different from all the rest was the forms and the glazes together. He was a real classicist, and he was really the only one who controlled what went on. The Coopers were completely different. The Coopers were making a wild range of stuff, and they were double dipping and triple dipping them with all these wild colors. I think the wonderful thing about Mr. Busbee is that he didn't give in to these thousands of forms and colors. He stuck with a very limited group of shapes and a limited palette. He translated a lot of the old jar forms very easily into Chinese forms. That classical sense he had was amazing at a time when the potters had found out how to order all these different colors. If I'd been a potter I would have tried all these colors. Mr. Busbee kept control of that pottery in a way no other shop did. Thus, I think what Jugtown made is more distinctive and probably aesthetically superior to anyone else.

Another thing that the Busbees didn't do, the Busbees did not change the technology. They kept the old pug mill with the mule and the treadle wheel and the groundhog kiln. Those were the symbols of the handmade pot, the symbols of age and nostalgia and part of that authenticating strategy that they certainly had. That was, again, part of Mr. Busbee's classic restraint because more sophisticated kilns and clay preparation machinery were all available then. And he didn't do that.

He got a good person in Ben Owen. He had that eye for form. A lot of those old potters had it. Burlon Craig always used to tell me that the old timers knew the difference between a good form and a bad form, but when you are making utilitarian pottery you don't have the time to worry about perfect forms. You've got to knock that stuff out. If it holds five gallons, that's all you need. That's the point in that world, but the Busbees introduced a new world. They brought in a much more marked aesthetic sense that was always potentially there. The work of a Himer Fox or a Daniel Seagle is proof that the old utilitarian potters could make gorgeous looking pots. I've seen hundreds of pots marked with both names, and you hardly ever see

one that isn't almost always perfect. And not only the form but the glaze too. But most of the old potters couldn't waste time on that. But the Busbees took these young men and Ben Owen in particular, and gave them the time and the awareness to look at form really carefully.

Treadle kick-wheel in the turning room at Jugtown Pottery with examples of Jugtown wares displayed, ca. 1950s.

Edited by Douglas DeNatale from a transcript of an interview with Charles G. Zug III, Chapel Hill, North Carolina, January 14, 1993, by Sally Council.

Willliam Arthur Staley

William Arthur Staley has been a lifelong resident of the Seagrove community. On the day in 1917 when Jacques Busbee arrived in Seagrove, Mr. Staley carried Mr. Busbee on his wagon to the home of Steve Richardson, where Busbee found lodging.

I was born December the fifteenth, 1902. And I was ninety the fifteenth of December. And see, I'm going in my ninety-first year, I've done passed ninety. I've been living here seventy-two years. I reckon I was fifteen, sixteen years old when Mr. Busbee came to Seagrove on the train. He had a trunk, and a suitcase. He was wanting to find where people were making stoneware. And he said, "I know you've got first class potters down here, and I'm interested in getting pie plates so they can make money." Well they wouldn't take him there. They thought he was a German spy. Wouldn't nobody that would tell him. Seagrove is just a small little place, of course, but there wasn't nobody to bring him.

He said, "I've got money to pay." So Mr. Parks, the depot agent, he said, "Yeah, I'll find you someone." Well, I had come to Seagrove with a load of cross ties, Mr. Parks said, "He'll carry you back." See, I'd been working ever since I could. My papa died when I was young, and children back then had to work. So I said I'd bring him over to Mr. Steve Richardson's.

So he said to me, "Well, you know, what if I get over there and I can't get nowhere?" And I said, "Well, it might not be just like you want it, but I'll take you home with me, and see that nobody don't bother you." And he said, "Oh, I've got a friend now." But I don't know how come they all thought he was a German spy. He said he didn't come to harm nobody. He just wanted to help the country make some money.

So I put him on my wagon and brought him over to Mr. Steve Richardson's. He was running a store, but he was running a little ware shop—his son was—and Mr. Busbee wanted me to go over there, and that's where I put him off.

Well, when I got over to Mr. Richardson's, he wouldn't talk to Mr. Busbee. He took me round the side of the store, and said "What did you bring that German here for?" He asked me how come I brought him over there. And I said, "He wanted to get in touch with the people that were making ware." Stoneware, you know. And he said, "What if he's got all type of bombs or something in that trunk that'll blow this whole country?" Mr. Richardson and his wife, they stayed up a full night and watched it—'cause he was a German spy, you know.

As we come out on the road, Mr. Busbee said, "Well, you are the only friend I've got." And he said, "I'm just worried a little, would you just take a little drink with me?" And I said, "No sir, I thank you." And he said, "Do you drink?" And I said, "Well, no, sir." Well, he put his hand in his coat pocket and pulled out a handful of money—greenbacks— and he just handed me five or six or seven one-dollar bills.

The main thoroughfare of Seagrove, N.C., ca. 1934.

I said, "I don't charge you nothing." Well, he come on down the road, and he says, "You don't want money. Would you take a drink." And I said, "No, sir." But I said, "My mother keeps a little whiskey for medicine." Old folks used to keep a little quinine, a little whiskey, and mama would always make us some dewberry wine. So, he gave me the first pint of sealed whiskey I'd ever seen—back then we called it "Ordered Whiskey."

He left and I put the mules up, started carrying it home, and I met some of the community people. And they said, "Did you bring a stranger in this community to spend the night?" And I said, "Yes." And Mr. Lauren Brantley, the man I was working for, he said, "Give me that thing." And I gave it to him. He took that pint of whiskey to Coleridge, to Dr. Claude Haywood. And he said, "There ain't nothing the matter with this. It's got a government seal." He opened it, and Mr. Claude just pulled it back and turned it up and drunk about a third of it. They just about drunk it all! I worked for Mr. Claude, too, and he had a good heart.

I went home and I told mama, and I said, "Mr. Lauren took my whiskey and I didn't bring it to you." And she said, "Well if you'd come home! There ain't no German spy. That whiskey, it won't hurt nobody 'cause it was a United States label on it wasn't it?" "Yes, ma'am." Said, "He didn't bring that from no Germany."

After everybody got used to Mr. Busbee, they weren't scared of him. And then after he went out to Mr. Owen's and he put up a shop, I used to go by there. It was a pretty good bit before I seen him again, but he knowed my name just as good as if I'd told him. Whenever I went to Robbins, I'd come back by. He never did forget me. He always, he called me "his boy," said, "You was nice to me." And he always, he told me if I got a chance to cut cord wood and haul it over there, he said, "I'll pay you good."

I used to go up when Mrs. Owen's husband worked over there. We talked, but everybody's work went on. He'd laugh. He'd tell them about the old days. He said, "He wasn't scared of a German spy." See I wasn't afraid of nothing back then. He told me, "Well you weren't scared of me the first time you ever seen me." And I said, "I knowed you was a good man. I can tell a good man." I said, "Anything I can do for you, I'm yours. I'll help anybody that is some body."

And you know, he never did forget that. He said, "You're my friend." And I thought a lot of him, too. Anybody treats me nice, well, I got to treat them nice.

That's just the way it was.

Edited by Douglas DeNatale from a transcript of an interview with William Arthur Staley, Seagrove, North Carolina, January 13, 1993, by Sally Council.

Annie Cagle Teague & John Garrett Teague

Annie Cagle Teague, Pinehurst, North Carolina, and John Garrett Teague, Robbins, North Carolina. Annie Teague, presently in her nineties, is the widow of Charlie Teague, who was hired by Jacques Busbee around 1921 to be the first potter to work at Jugtown. Garrett is their only son.

AT: Before we married, Charlie worked at High Point, where he lived with his brother. That's where I met him. But after his appendix burst, he went to his mother's. After we got married, Charlie was working for his daddy, John Wesley Teague.

JGT: They had a pottery shop across the road from where Jim Teague's place is now. A cyclone come and set the house over. Never did find the top of the barn.

AT: Well, when Busbee came, he got all the information he could about pottery and went back to New York. Nobody was turning in the area but my husband when he came back. I used to cook for people who visited from up north. I'd cook what they wanted, and they wanted cornbread and greens.

JGT: She used to cook cornbread and pies in things daddy used to make. We've still got a set of stoneware cups and saucers he made.

AT: He made one with my initials on it.

JGT: He gave me a shaving mug I used for years, until I cleaned it and put it up.

Jacques Busbee and Charlie Teague packing pottery into barrels for shipment by train to New York City, ca. mid 1920s.

AT: I never did know much about what was going on at Jugtown because I was always cooking and cleaning for folks. I couldn't do my work and watch after what the Busbees were up to all the time. But I do remember that Foxie Grandpa.

JGT: That was Carl Shultz. Foxie Grandpa was his nickname.

AT: He stayed many a month, I believe, for long visits. He's the one that Garrett would trot along after, and he wore a panama hat. Once he turned his hat inside out and picked some berries, and put them in it. Then he brought them to the house and wanted me to bake a pie. I told him I didn't have time to bake a pie then. I said, "You can eat

them with sugar and cream on them." So that's the way they ate them. But I don't remember too many of the people who visited. So many came.

Back then, my mother was weaving on an old loom. The Busbees went around everywhere and bought up spinning wheels and looms.

JGT: Mr. Busbee loved all that stuff.

AT: He sure did. Anyways, they shipped all the ware from down here in barrels to New York City. I remember Mr. Busbee often would bring a book or a magazine for me from Robbins when he'd come. Eventually Dewey Teague,

Charlie's brother, helped them build the kiln in Jugtown. And Ben Owen boarded with us until he married.

JGT: Mr. Busbee mixed the glazes. When they turned the ware, they had to sit it on the planks to dry.

AT: When Mrs. Busbee came down you had to follow her around. She'd sit pottery on the edge of everything. I remember that when they had the party to celebrate Jugtown pottery in the Southern Exposition, they roasted a small hog. A colored man, McCarthage, did the cooking. They had all kinds of pies.

JGT: What I remember about Mr. Busbee was he wore them little knee britches. At Jugtown, a Reader man ground the clay. One cup is all I ever turned. I don't know what happened to it. They must have thrown it away. See, I was small, real small. And by the time I'd got bigger to think of anything, we'd moved to Robbins and daddy was in Smithfield. So I didn't think about it then.

AT: In the early thirties, Charlie went to work at Smithfield, and would come over to Robbins now and then. About two years later he joined us there. I'd moved to Robbins and went to work in a rayon mill. I worked there twenty years before I quit. Charlie worked at the mill too.

JGT: But he didn't work there but a little while before he died. He died of pneumonia in 1938, the last week of November.

AT: Working on that water, clay and stuff, a potter don't have a long life. But you know, after we left Jugtown, every newspaper article I'd read about the place would make me so mad. His daddy, Garrett's daddy, is the one that was the main potter there at the beginning. Those articles never did say that.

Charlie Teague glazing pots, ca. 1930, Jugtown Pottery.

Edited by Jane Przybysz from a transcript of an interview with Annie Cagle Teague and John Garrett Teague, Pinehurst, North Carolina, January 28, 1993, by Jill Severn, Jane Przybysz, and Pam Owens.

Lucille H. Owen

Lucille H. Owen, Seagrove, North Carolina, is the widow of Ben Owen, who in the late twenties became the main potter at Jugtown.

Mrs. Busbee was judging a fair in Lexington, North Carolina in 1915, the year I was born. She was the head of the art division in the North Carolina's Woman's Club, and she was asked to come to Lexington to judge this county fair. A farmer was displaying his apples in a bright orange pie plate as she described it—what was then called a dirt dish. And she asked the farmer who made this container. The farmer said, "Well I really don't know. I bought it down here at the hardware. They told me I had to put my apples in a container, and I didn't have a box or anything, and I just went down there to get me one of these dirt dishes." He said, "Don't you think they look pretty in it?"

Now, I wasn't with Mrs. Busbee at the time, of course, but I heard her tell that many, many times when I would drive her different places to make talks into Virginia, South Carolina, all over the state. But anyway, that's what she said. And he did not know who made it, so she said, "I could not get the blue ribbons on fast enough to get down to the hardware store to get me one." And when she got there, they had one left and two little "demijohns"—a little tiny jug that they used to put vinegar on the table. She got the two little "demijohns" and the bright orange plate. He told her that they were made by a man by the name of Rufus Owen, and come up here by a "wagoneer," packed in straw. And that was Ben's father who lived at Whynot, North Carolina—well, Whynot was their post office though they lived about four miles away from Whynot.

She wrote an article once for *The State* magazine, and she concluded it by saying that "she and Mr. Busbee set sail in a bright orange pie plate rather than a pea green boat, and lived happily ever after." That's the beginning of their business really. That winter they had decided that they would go up to New York just for the winter "to do the city," to go to the theater, to the opera, to the museum, and just "do the city." Mr. Busbee had studied art in New York. So in the course of it, she decided to open a little tearoom down in Greenwich Village on Washington Square.

So they sold their home in Raleigh in order to underwrite that. And she took her pie plate with her and several little things she had bought as well as the "demijohns." And she needed some chicken pie plates in which to make her "Chicken pot pie," as she called it, and several other pieces. So Mr. Busbee came to Whynot looking for Rufus Owen, and that was exciting!

He found out he could not get to Whynot on the train—it was just a rural post office—but he could get to Seagrove which was near. When he got off the train in Seagrove with his two trunks, he asked the fellow that kept the depot, "How can I get to Rufus Owen the potter who is at Whynot?" And this was right before World War I, and he was not dressed locally and he didn't speak the dialect, so the station master sort of suspected Mr. Busbee. He didn't know what to tell him, but he said, "Maybe if you'll go over here to the "General Store" they can tell you." So he went across the highway to the "General Store," and he told the merchant that the station master had told him to come over and find out how he could find Rufus Owen, a potter.

There was a group of men in there, like there usually was in those country stores, talking, and they began to punch each other saying, "What does he want with Rufus Owen?" So no one would tell him, and one of them said, "I tell you, I think he's a spy. He doesn't speak like our people." And in the course of it, this colored man, Arthur Staley, after a little bit interrupted and said, "Well, I passed Mr. Rufus's shop coming up here, and I can take you down there." Then he said, "I think I know where you can stay. There is a farmer down there, Mr. Richardson, who has a nice home, and I believe he'll let you stay there overnight." Mr. Busbee took Arthur's offer. They loaded Mr. Busbee's two trunks on the wagon and went down the road.

Mr. Busbee said he'd be happy if Mr. Richardson would let him stay. He said he'd let him see in his trunks. So Arthur said that he had opened the trunks and I asked Arthur, "What was in the trunks?" And he said, "Well, books and his clothing," and said he had something, little packets like that, and he said Mr. Richardson says to him, "What you got in these little packages?" And Mr. Busbee said, "They're glazes. I have seen that they have possibilities, and I thought maybe Mr. Owen might be interested in trying some new glazes." So he says, "All right, Arthur take his two trunks off and put them on the porch."

After they got the trunks on the porch, he gave Harris Richardson—the boy was sixteen years old—a pint of Canadian whiskey. Arthur said, "We looked at it," and said, "We didn't know—we'd never seen any Canadian whiskey." Later they decided they would take it over to Dr. Hayworth who lived at Coleridge and let him tell them what it was. And Arthur said, "You should have seen him smack his lips." He said, "There's nothing the matter with this. This is good Canadian whiskey; they can get it in New York." So Arthur says, "Harris and I were scared to death he was going to drink it all and we weren't going to get the taste of it."

Anyway, in the course of it, Mr. Richardson let him stay and he found Mr. Owen—"Mr. Rufus"—as Arthur called him. After Mr. Busbee found him and told him he wanted him to make pots to be shipped from Seagrove to Mrs. Busbee's little tearoom in the Village on Washington Square in New York—the dirt dish pie plates, chicken pie plates, and some other things—dome-lidded stew crocks, and mugs, coffee mugs, etc…

When Mr. Busbee found Rufus Owen, Ben had just finished high school. He wasn't going away to work in the furniture factories as his two brothers had done. He stayed on to work with his father. Mr. Busbee saw that Ben's father and Ben and his older brother were doing well, and had art qualities. Mr. Busbee said, "I saw that Ben had talent." So he asked Ben about helping him get a pottery started. So Ben decided he would.

Now they opened the shop in 1923. He first leased the land from a Mr. Scott—Henry Scott—and eventually he bought it. Ben would go down there—he and Mr. Busbee shared a room at the Henry Scotts'. They built the kilns and they built the work area, and they built the shop, but they didn't get the log cabin built, and they lived with the Justice of the Peace, Henry Scott, right close to where they were building the shop. So Ben really was there from day one. Charlie Teague came to Jugtown and worked there after, you know, they got started and needed some more help. But he didn't work out. They got the shop ready first and began to make pottery. You see, Mr. Busbee was shipping it up to New York on the train in barrels packed in straw. Mrs. Busbee had converted a section in her little tearoom where she sold the pottery.

Mrs. Busbee continued to operate her little tearoom till 1928, so from 1923 to 1928, he and Mr. Busbee closed the shop in the fall right after Thanksgiving—that was the custom here whenever the pottery would freeze in their shop. They just closed the shop until spring, and he and Mr. Busbee would go to New York and Mr. Busbee would take Ben and get on the train and go to Boston or to Yale University or down to Washington. He was giving Ben that training. They studied in the museums there in New York, and one spring, Ben was fortunate enough to get to go to art school. Ben said that Mr. Busbee had good rapport with the people who were directors of the museums and they gave him a lot of time. They even went to New Orleans one time. I heard Ben express how thankful he was that he did that, because it gave him opportunities he'd never had, and he never would have had.

That's how he got acquainted with the oriental masters. That's how they began to make the oriental shapes and designs. Up until that time the area had made the utilitarian type things: jugs and churns and big crocks and little "demi-johns." Ben's family didn't seem to mind at all. They felt he was getting an opportunity. He came back and brought it back to his brothers. His work influenced them, too. In fact, he introduced oriental shapes to the area, because he absolutely was fascinated with them. And in the evenings over at the Busbees, Mr. Busbee had lots of art books and he and Ben studied those and would think about developing new shapes or new glazes. Ben said, "The Busbees were like parents to me. I went to live with Mr. Busbee when I was eighteen years old, and it was just like family."

Mr. Busbee taught him to play bridge, and they used to love to play bridge. Ben was a great reader, and he and Mr. Busbee would read and discuss what they were reading. And he did a lot of driving for them. Ben did demonstrations in Louisiana, Washington, different places. It was in Chapel Hill during the Dogwood Festival in 1928, when Ben was doing a demonstration, that he was declared a Master Potter by the University.

I came to Robbins to teach in the fall of 1935, and then I met Ben and we were married in 1937. Years ago they used to have what we called rural schools—community schools that were sponsored by the church. I lived in the girls dormitory of the Elise

Ben Owen enjoys dinner with Jacques and Juliana Busbee, ca. 1940s.

Jacques Busbee stands with his iris garden at Jugtown, ca. 1940s. Jacques Busbee was an avid gardener who raised champion irises at Jugtown.

eight o'clock a.m., and come home about five p.m. Sometimes I'd go over and help Mrs. Busbee. She'd have groups coming, and she'd prepare food for them, and I would help her. They were very interesting people, they really were. And they did a lot of good things. I know she saw to it that they got a school over there in that neighborhood. They were good citizens.

They got both my children interested in arranging flowers. Mrs. Busbee would get them to go down in the woods with her to get the wildflowers. She would give Jane lessons in flower arranging, and today she's an International Flower Show Judge. And Mr. Busbee grew irises. His garden was the prettiest thing—he began with white irises, then went all the way around, and then came back, and he called the last part of it the black iris. It was a purple that was so dark it looked black. She had all these beautiful plants all year round—see, he had a hot house-type thing so plants would not freeze in the winter time. Their house was very, very interesting. They had lots of books, and the curtains in the house were made of a material that was woven by some of the people who did weaving in that area.

So things went along real good. Mr. Busbee kept his garden and he would glaze the pots, and Ben and the outside workers—people who did the firing and that type of thing—they stayed busy. Then Mr. Busbee died of a heart-attack, and Ben stayed on and kept things going until John Maré wanted to buy the property. Mrs. Busbee had gotten senile. It was pitiful, it really was.

Maré tried to get Ben to go down to Southern Pines and open a pottery for him down there. And of course, Ben wasn't going to do that. He said, "I can't leave Mrs. Busbee. Somebody has to take care of her." What I would do to see that she didn't starve, I'd get home from school and I'd prepare our evening meal and when I got it finished I would carry a plate to her.

Ben was trying to get it fixed so that we could have the authority to take care of her. But it just didn't work out. John Maré came in and got her to sign this contract which she did and he filed it. Then he came and took over. It was right sad, and Ben just couldn't work with him. He told Ben how much "stuff" they had to produce. You see, Ben and Mr. Busbee weren't so concerned about how many pieces they made—it was how well it was made. Maré began to tell Ben about how many thousand pieces they had to turn out, and Ben says, "I can't work with him at all." Mrs. Busbee said to him, "Ben, you can't leave. You and Lucille are going to carry on this place when I'm gone." And he said, "Mrs. Busbee, you sold it." And she couldn't understand that, she really couldn't.

Academy. One time, one of the teachers and I were coming home from school, and Ben was going in to get his hair cut. One of the teachers that was teaching with me, Catherine MacDonald was her name, she knew Ben, and she introduced me to him. Another time, three of us teachers had stopped at a little restaurant uptown, and Ben came in, and Catherine says, "Come sit with us." She introduced us again, and he says, "Oh I met Miss Harris—don't you remember when I met you on the street over here?" And I said "Oh yes, you did, didn't you?" So that was that.

He had just bought this property here, and he had moved into his log cabin. So, they wanted to go out and see the log cabin. So we did, and then when we got ready to go home, he put me in the front seat beside him and the other two in the back seat. When we got back to the "dorm," he helped them out of the car, gentleman that he was, and he says to me, "You just stay here a minute." So when he got them to the door he asked me if I would like him to carry me home on Friday. I told him that would be real nice, yes, I'd appreciate that. So he carried me home and that was the beginning of our relationship.

I'd go home most every weekend. I lived over in Candor. Ben would come and take me home on Friday night and come back Saturday night, and we'd go out some place and eat, or go to some place and dance. He was a wonderful dancer. We'd go down to Southern Pines or Pinehurst or up to Asheboro or Greensboro, places where you could have dinner and dance. Pinehurst was our favorite though, the Carolina Hotel. You'd have dinner, then you'd go in the ballroom and dance. It was real nice. On Sunday, he would come and carry me back to the dormitory. In the spring, we began to talk about marriage and during Easter vacation we were married in Rockingham Methodist Church.

We first lived in that little log cabin. He didn't work here. All his work was at Jugtown. He'd go out about

Her friends all supported Ben. They thought it was terrible. But, as Ben said, "I made the pottery there and I can make it here." So he had him a stamp made saying "Ben Owen: Master Potter." It's really wonderful how much they supported Ben. Several said, "You know Ben, it was a blessing." But Ben never felt that way about it. Because as he said, "Mrs. Busbee's family to me and I want to see that she's taken care of." That's what he worried about. He said, "Those four or five acres of land I'm not too concerned about, but I'm concerned about her." And he was really, surely was. He said, "When I left, that was the end of Jugtown as far as I'm concerned."

We had built this building for the children, "to play in," as Ben said. The family gave him their father's potters wheel, and he put that in there. So when everything took the turn that it did, we tore down one of the tobacco barns over on the farm and built this part, and he took the old chicken house that we weren't using any more and got that cleaned up as the storage area. That's where he began, in there. He built two kilns—one's an earthenware kiln and the other's a stoneware kiln. And before he really got going he had orders that he couldn't have filled in a year. Then later he just had to give it up. His hands and his whole body were so affected with arthritis.

Ben III was such a pleasure to his grandfather. He went to school here, next door and he'd come here after school. His grandfather's health had gotten so bad that he wasn't able to make pots any more. He'd sit in the chair with his grand father, and they'd talk. When Ben was about nine years old, he suggested to his grandfather that he go out to the shop and let him see if he could make some pots, and I remember Ben Senior said, "We don't have any clay, Ben." He said, "Granddaddy, you got a lot of clay." Grandfather's answer was, "Honey, it's dry, you can't work with it. But I'll get you some." So the next day before school was out, Ben said, "Let's go up to Joe's"—Joe was his brother who also was a potter—"And let's see if I can't get Ben some clay." So we went up there and got him some, and Granddaddy was ready when Ben III got home that after-noon from school. So he had his glass of milk and a cookie, and they went on out to the shop.

Some of the first things that Ben III made, like his candle holder and his first teapot, were real cute. I was washing the dishes when he made the first candle holder. He came to the back door and says, "Grandmother, come out here. I have something I want to show you." I couldn't wait to get my hands dry to get out there. And he said, "What do you think of this?" And I said, "Ben, I think that's real pretty." I said, "Did you ever see your grandfather make one?" He said, "No, Grandmother, I didn't. But I've looked at it, and felt it, and studied it, and I decided I'd try to make me one." I said, "Let's take it in to let Granddaddy see it." Granddaddy was sitting there in the recliner, and we brought it in, and you should have seen the look on his face. You could just see him beaming.

Today, Ben III has a B.S. degree in Art and Ceramic Design from East Carolina University, Greenville, North Carolina. He continues to make pottery in the Original Ben Owen Pottery on N.C. Hwy. 705, Route 2, Seagrove, North Carolina, 27341. He also adds shapes he has designed.

Just recently he was invited to do a show and demonstration in Atlanta, Georgia and in Columbia, South Carolina.

Edited by Douglas DeNatale from transcripts of interviews with Lucille H. Owen, Seagrove, North Carolina, September 25, 1993, by Sally Council.

41

Melvin L. Owens

Melvin L. Owens is the son of J. H. Owen and the father of Vernon Owens. He has been a potter all his life and has operated the Owens Pottery with the help of his family for more than fifty years. Over the years, Mr. Owens also helped out at Jugtown hauling lumber and building kilns.

When I was young, there wasn't too many potters. It was hard work. You had to go out and dig your clay, haul it with a wagon, and drive it with a mule or horse. I've hauled clay seven miles from here with a horse and wagon. It was all hard labor, standing and kicking a wheel. I've been making on the wheel about fifty-seven years and I'm the oldest Owens man in my generation. I had five brothers and every one of them learned to make pots. The business was started in 1910.

My daddy, J. H. Owen, learned under a man by the name of Paschal Marable. Jason Miller owned a pottery shop and he had a big farm and he married my daddy's aunt. And this old man was there making pottery and my daddy got to going over and stay with them, visiting, and he went to work making it. He said he was seventeen years old when he learned.

When Mr. Busbee first came down from New York he went over in Chatham County to some people named Fox. Then he went up about six miles to a Richardson that made pottery. The old man Richardson didn't make it, but he hired somebody to come and do it. You see, there were so many pottery shops back then that the people owned it actually didn't make any pottery. They had somebody else coming in to make it. The Richardson's stuff was so rough Mr. Busbee didn't like it. The Richardsons sent him to my daddy in 1917, the

year I was born. So he came down to my daddy and he stayed right here. He boarded with my uncle that built Jugtown—my mamma's brother, J. H. Scott—for, I'm going to say six years. I'm sure he stayed on with them a little while after he took Jugtown. From 1921 to 1923, my uncle probably built what he built at Jugtown—the log building, down where Vernon worked and where the old clay mill is setting. Then he built the sale room, the little log cabin out there. Then he built the dwelling house.

My father was working for Mr. Busbee all the time he was staying with my uncle from 1917 to 1923. The Busbees got what he had made for them here, and took it down to Jugtown to finish it. Daddy never had the privilege to work for the Busbees at Jugtown because he died at fifty-seven years old the year they moved down there.

The year he died was also the first year he demonstrated at the fair in Pinehurst. I could take you to the old building. I went there with him and he had his wheel set up. And

Ernest Williamson [left] and Rancie Moore [right] glazing wares at Jugtown Pottery, ca. 1940s. Both Rancie Moore and Ernest Williamson did outside work at Jugtown from the late twenties through the 1940s.

then he had another space that he displayed pottery. He would go to Winston-Salem, probably around the Old Salem there, and they would have a fair and he would go up there. I think maybe one time he went to Highpoint. But by that time, T-model cars had come out, and they had cars to travel in.

Charlie Teague started at Jugtown. But Mr. Busbee also had Robert Scott, Jason Reeder, Herbert Scott, not all at one time, but he had them work. Then he had Hurley Hussey, Arthur Davis, a lot of them around here. Most of them just done the outside work—got the clay, ground the clay, took it to the kiln and put it in. Mr. Busbee did the painting and decorating, working five or six days a week. He mixed the glazes himself, nobody else did that for him. That was his job. His wife helped him for several years, but she was more the salesman.

Ben Owen went there as a boy, say about seventeen years old. Charlie Teague and Benny grew up right together. Before they married and left, their homes were not too far apart. Charlie Teague might have helped give Bennie the job.

If the pots Ben made didn't come out right, Mr. Busbee would take them and break them. Right down back on this side of the old house down there where Vernon lives, there's a pile of pottery they'd just fill big ditches up with. But they could still make a living because back then they didn't have much overhead expense. Wood was a dollar a cord. They'd charge you a dollar to dig a pick-up truck load of clay, and the people who owned the land got fifty cents. There wasn't any expense in it. They could sell a piece of pottery for two dollars then and clear a dollar and a half after paying for the materials and labor in it. Some potteries paid potters by the piece, but Jugtown paid by the day.

I helped the Busbees all I could and they depended on me. They depended on me to haul all their wood for about twenty years. They kept a small truck and most of the time I had a large truck. We worked together just like I've also worked with other potters' places. I'm not jealous over nobody.

Mr. Busbee was a nice person. There wasn't very many people around here that liked him, but as far as I'm concerned, me and him was real friends. He was just a different person than the southern people were. He came from Raleigh. That's where they both came from. Mr. Busbee's father was a judge, but Mr. Busbee liked to be on his own. He came down and started into shipping pottery. I had one brother older than I am and they'd take the stuff down to Robbins. What they had packed up in barrels and boxes they'd take to the depot and put it on the train. At that time, my daddy made pots with orange and grey salt

glaze with a blue in it. My mother made clay chickens. This here is a lamp. It looks funny to be a lamp. I'm going to tell you how they done it. See, it's sitting up on four legs? There's a hole in the bottom of that and they drop the cord for the light, but there was a metal stand that went up in the center of this thing. They called them porch lights and the switch went on top here on the iron rod. I think Mr. Busbee came up with the design. But my daddy worked making it. There ain't no stamp or anything on it.

In the 1930s they got to making that art glaze. I think that comes out of Virginia. One time there was thirty-five

W. Boyce Yow holding one of his famous clay catfishes. Boyce Yow has worked off and on at Jugtown throughout his career, first for the Busbees in the 1940s and 1950s, then later, for Pamela and Vernon Owens during the 1980s. He died in 1986. .

potters in the Shenandoah Valley, and my brother and I, back in the early 1930s, we hauled pottery up to Luray and Winchester, all up in there. We made a lot of trips. The last place was closed out up there in 1935. I'm sure that's where a lot of this art glaze started.

I just thought the world of Mr. Busbee. He came by one Saturday in about 1945, and talked about me coming down to Jugtown and building him a new kiln. And then he had to go in the hospital and he died. But I built his kilns for him—along with Rancie Moore who did outside work for him.

Mrs. Busbee was just as nice as I've ever met. She never met a stranger. At first she ran the studio up there in New York. But she moved down probably in 1925 or 1926. Charlie Teague and his wife lived down at Jugtown with him for at least two years before Mrs. Busbee came down. I always liked to go down there and eat with them. I liked her cooking. She'd make soup and baked chicken. And I liked to sit and talk to her. That was even before I was married.

Melvin Owens works on the kiln at Jugtown with his son Bob's assistance. John Maré examines a burned brick from the kiln with Juliana Busbee, ca. 1959.

Vernon's a good potter, not because he's my son, but because when people ask him how he learned this or how he knows that, he says, "I just know what my daddy does." I hope all these other potters' places can keep going. The more competition looks like we have, the better business we've got.

I didn't go to work for Jugtown like my dad did because I wanted to stay here. My daddy left it and all my brothers married off and our mama lived thirty years after our father died, so I kind of stayed around to take care of her, help her.

When she was young, Mrs. Busbee went back to Raleigh probably every week. She never did drive a car. She had people at work do her driving. Back then they were making fifteen dollars a month. You could hire a chauffeur back then. Jugtown finally closed down in 1959 because Mrs. Busbee got old, and though her mind was still good, she would forget things. Another man bought the place, John Maré. And then Ben quit and left down there. He wouldn't work for that man. He didn't like him.

Then Ben and some more people put a lawsuit against John Maré for buying Jugtown. I had the keys to the place for over fifteen months. John Maré gave them to me to look after the place cause they put a restraining order on him. He had hired me and Bobby, my boy down there at Jugtown. He'd just sign the checks and give them to me to build him two new kilns. So we were down there working and they sent a deputy sheriff up there and told us we couldn't work any more. So I become independent and I said, "Who's going to stop me?" And he said, "Didn't you know there's a restraining order on this place?" I said, "I don't know, but Bobby and I have got a lot of labor in this thing, too." I said, "You just stop and think about that." He said, "You can't do no more work down here." I said, "You can't stop me." And they didn't try to stop me. I went ahead and finished it.

John Maré was a good man. He was a business man. He wanted everything done and done his way, and I liked him. He had real funny ways, but I still liked him and he liked me.

When the lawsuit was settled, Maré hired Vernon to go down there and work for him. He was around eighteen years old. He learned standing watching me turn. He didn't like to go to school because he miss being with me. He went to turning when he was about eight years old, as quick as he got large enough to stand up to the wheel.

When she died, I had to buy out ten brothers and sisters. That was back in the 1940s when I started buying it, and then it was about 1960 before I bought all the rest of it. But I had the home down there, I had the shops, everything.

I turned every bit of this over to my son in 1975. I'm not rich, but I don't have to get up and come down here every morning like I did from 1937 to 1975. We had five wheels in here at one time—me, my son-in-law, and two of my girls, and another man, we had five of them.

Sometimes I think back fifty and sixty years ago to how things was back then. But I don't want to go back there and live. I don't want to have to jump up in the night and run way out to an outside toilet. And I don't want to have to come down here and do like I had to do fifty-seven years ago when I started. I don't care a thing about that. We can run more clay through now in two hours than I could in twelve hours, the way we did it back then.

There's more art to making pottery today than there was then. I don't call myself an artist because I don't decorate. I just make the pottery and put my name on the bottom of it. But I'll tell you what I'm going to do. Vernon made a salt glaze jug and put a lot of old people that he had known on it. I'm going to make one some day about this tall and this big around, draw lines and think of all the old potters that I can remember, and put each one of their names in rows.

Edited by Jane Przybysz from a transcript of an interview with Melvin L.Owens, Seagrove, North Carolina, January 12, 1994, by Douglas DeNatale.

New Pottery For Connoisseurs

Strap-handled platter artfully displayed on a chair.

Woodrow Pruett and William Bridges

Woodrow Pruett made his first acquaintance with Juliana Busbee through his life-long friend, William Bridges and Bridges's mother, Emma. Pruett and Bridges were frequent visitors and correspondents with Juliana, who referred to them as intimate members of her "Universal Family." Pruett and Bridges donated two significant collections of Jugtown pottery to St. John's Gallery in Wilmington, North Carolina, and to the North Carolina Museum of History in Raleigh, North Carolina.

WP: I first learned about Jugtown pottery in about 1953. Ben Williams, curator of the museum in Raleigh, showed me a pair of Jugtown candlesticks. I've always been a lover of candlesticks, and the design and beauty of these . . . well, I lost my mind. He wanted a certain price for them and I agreed.

In the meantime, Billy Bridges and I decided we would go to Jugtown and seek out Juliana Busbee. I was living in Virginia, but I'd spend weekends down here in Lumberton. We got Jugtown candlesticks from her at a price ten times cheaper from Ben. We immediately became warm friends of Juliana. Her interest in books and the arts was right up my alley. She was one of the most wonderful women I've ever met. Physically she was not pretty; the beauty was all within—great intelligence, great sense of humor, great sense of duty. I just fell in love with her the first time I saw her. She was a beautiful, beautiful selective snob.

WB: But never unkind. She would never hurt anybody.

WP: We'd go there maybe every two weeks. I would go to Winston-Salem once a month, and I'd go by and cook her cabbage and salami for lunch. She ate it just like she was starved to death. She said, "Woodrow, you remind me very much of the man in Lorna Doone who swam the river every day to cook for Lorna." She knew books. She knew the classics.

Often on Saturday night, we would have dinner with her. She'd have dinner parties most every Saturday night. Artists, college professors from Chapel Hill were there often.

Cleta Rich was one of Juliana's best friends. She was from Asheboro and spent a lot of time at Jugtown.

WB: Clarence Thompson was a lifelong friend of the Busbees and after Jacques died, she'd always include him on Thanksgiving and Christmas dinner because he was alone. Juliana knew so many people.

WP: Most of them were these young students at the University of North Carolina. The friends that she liked best of all were younger people with creative minds who were controversial in their thoughts so she could debate with them.

WB: She liked Baker Wynn. He was from Raleigh and taught at N.C. State. He was a good friend of hers, and so was Isabelle Henderson. She was a very good friend.

Juliana Busbee sits at her dining room table at Jugtown, circa 1940s.

WP: Isabelle painted portraits. At any rate, Juliana always asked me to be host, even if seven or eight other people were eating there, and one night she put me to carving opossum. There I was with my back to a fireplace that was about to burn me up, and my face burning up from trying to carve that opossum. She never let me forget it.

After dinner, we'd wash the dishes in two punch bowls at the dinner table. One was for soapy water, and the one next to it had plain water. Each guest was given a cup towel and they would just wash the dishes and put them right back in place and keep good conversation going.

She nicknamed me "Omar" because of my love for poetry. But when we met Mary Hambidge in Rabun Gap, Georgia, she started calling me Omar, so Juliana went back to Woodrow. Juliana Busbee had many of her dresses, very primitive dresses, designed by this woman at Rabun Gap.

Juliana never wore silk stockings, which was marvelous beyond words. But the time she went to Raleigh to the reception in her honor, she had on high heel shoes. I thought I would laugh myself to death because Juliana was laughing her head off about it.

As a child she'd kept a copy of *Evangeline* in her pocket. She'd go down by the riverside and read *Evangeline* until she cried her eyes out. When she felt the curtain was descending, she gave me her copy of it. She thought the two words—primeval forest—that's often in that book, were the two most beautiful words in the English language.

When Juliana fell in love with Jacques Busbee, he was making no money and she had no money. She was never impressed with money. She wanted style. She wanted class. She wanted sophistication. They were both from old families in Raleigh, North Carolina. She was a Royster, which was a very prominent family there. According to Juliana, her mother would have an Italian dinner party. She would serve only Italian food, and they would speak in Italian. Another time she would serve a German dinner and they would speak in German.

WB: They were well-educated people.

WP: She only went to New York to open that tea shop so she could peddle Jugtown pottery. There were not enough people in that area of North Carolina interested in the beauty of this stuff. She thought if she went to New York, and found a sophisticated market, her product would sell. She stayed there a few years, and talked to all the people who came to her shop to eat soup and purchase Jugtown pottery. But Juliana didn't say much about her days at the tearoom. Like all discerning people, she was not a name dropper.

When her family found out that she had decided to move to the backwoods of Moore County, they were horrified. But she closed the tearoom in New York and came back down to North Carolina because she was head over heels in love with Jacques Busbee. He was down here in North Carolina alone, and she wanted to be with him. She thought Jacques Busbee was a great man. He was a great artist, had a great sense of humor, and was a very intelligent man. They did a great deal of reading. They were born to be with each other. When she put his ashes in one of these urns, and kept it in her bedroom on her chest of drawers, people sort of frowned at that. But after she died, she had her ashes placed in that same urn to be spread there at Jugtown.

She liked a primitive way of life and Jugtown was primitive. She knew how to cook and how to keep a house beautifully, primitive though it was. She would use burnt orange

curtains, and she would have no rugs on the floor whatsoever. It would just be pine boards. And there was no television in the house and no telephone.

In pottery, Juliana wanted simplicity—like the burnt orange pie plate. It's a beautiful piece, but it can be used. She was not impressed with anything that had fancy attachments. She also did not like pompous people. One time a woman came to Jugtown, and said to Juliana, "Oh, Mrs. Busbee, tell me about this little flower. Isn't it a lovely thing?" Mrs. Busbee said, "Yes, they call this an aristocrat flower." "Well, why?" asked this woman. "Well, you have to get down and if you're an aristocratic person, you'll get the most glorious aroma in this whole wide world from it." The woman got down on her knees and she busted her stockings and probably two or three stays in her corset, and she got up and said, "I'm overcome with the beautiful aroma." And Juliana Busbee gave me a wink, and an hour later said, "You know the flower didn't have a bit of aroma."

Another time, we went to fetch Juliana to take her to a big reception at the Governor's Mansion, and when she came out she had her dress on wrong side out. I said, "Juliana, your dress is on wrong side out." And she said, "Omar, does that really matter?" I said, "No, Juliana, it doesn't." That gives you a perfect example of her character. When she reached the reception, the Governor and the whole receiving line broke up and got around her. All of them spent the rest of the evening with her.

She was just a marvelous, marvelous woman. On one occasion, she said, "Woodrow, I had the most glorious weekend in this whole wide world. Two of my friends from Chapel Hill came and fetched me to Raleigh for some function and en route we stopped at that store where you can buy all that good stuff the Baptists will pass up. She was talking about the liquor store. She loved her toddy and she held it beautifully.

She called me a philanderer. I got a letter once from her addressed to Mr. Philanderer, West Atlantic Street, Emporia, Virginia, and you know, the mailman delivered it.

She was one of a kind in this world. She just loved for you to sit there and quote Emily Dickinson. She loved to quote Whitman's line about "lilacs last. . ." What is the thing she used to always say about her and Jacques and Jugtown? "We were like the owl and the pussycat who went to sea in a beautiful pie plate instead of a pea green boat, and it landed on shores just as amazing. . ."

Edited by Jane Przybysz from a transcript of an interview with Woodrow Pruett and William Bridges, Lumberton, North Carolina, August 13, 1993, by Jill Severn and Douglas DeNatale.

Mrs. Paul L. Cox (Louise)

Louise Cox, together with her late husband Paul, began collecting Jugtown pottery in the early 1950s.

When we first started going down into the area, we went directly to Jugtown. My husband and I were married in 1949, and we didn't start going down until 1950, 1951, 1952, somewhere along in there. See, our first knowledge about Jugtown was that the Busbees realized that the farmers in the area needed some other kind of an outlet, needed something to improve their way of living. So they started the pottery to make utility pieces for the farmers and people living around the Jugtown area. Plates and cups and saucers and pots and bowls, and whatever they needed in their dining rooms and kitchens. And, I don't remember how it was that Mrs. Busbee started going to New York and when they started shipping stuff to New York. I don't remember how that came about. That is another story.

Her idea was good, it was to give the farmers and the people in the area something else to do. And I feel sure that with her background, she felt she was enhancing the quality of life for the farmers, trying to upgrade them. Which it did, because some of them left the farms and started potting.

Then people like us would start going down, and they'd say, "How much is this piece?" And she'd say, "Well, whatever you want to give me for it." See, that was the very beginning of how they started out of the little shop, I think. Then, after that, the Coles and other potters started making it a big retailing business. But see, that wasn't Jugtown. That was pottery, but it was a different kind. You know a lot of people say that when you talk about Jugtown, you're talking about the Coles and all these other potters. That's to me the Jugtown area. Jugtown proper is the little place where the Busbees lived and had the shop. To me—that is Jugtown.

The first time that we went was on a Saturday. We left in the morning about ten. When lunch time came, we looked around to find something to eat. We could not find a place anywhere—except one service station—without coming all the way back to Asheboro. So, from then on we always brown-bagged a lunch and took our cooler with drinks. We'd open the trunk and just eat out of the car. As the years went along, we would be riding down or coming back, and we'd see a little sign of another potter, and we'd go into that area and back and forth.

We would go down and go into the Jugtown shop, and, of course, I was real curious. I would ask about Mrs. Busbee.

See, she just would not let anybody into her house. She was more or less a recluse for a long time. I had heard about one time when this friend of mine went with some friends of hers, and she had her children with her, and her little girl needed to go to the bathroom. She asked the girl in the shop if there was a bathroom anywhere. She said, no, it was in Mrs. Busbee's house but she wouldn't let anybody go in there. But her special friends, she would let them come in just any time.

But we went down one time, and it was a real pretty Saturday, and we parked in the little lot there and looked up on the Busbee porch. And Mrs. Busbee was outside standing on the porch. So I just said, "Hello. Good morning, Mrs. Busbee." She said, "Come over and visit with me." Well, we were flabbergasted! So Paul and I walked over.

We'd seen her before at a distance, but this was the first time she had ever spoken to or tried to be friendly with me, an outsider. So we walked over to the porch, and she said, "Well, come in and visit." It didn't impress my husband because he had probably not heard as much about the Busbees as I had in talking with different people. So we went in, and then she started telling us about things that she had. She walked into their sitting room where there was this old wicker furniture, and up on this mantle was stuff, and she had a fire in the fireplace. She was telling us just out of the clear about where some of this stuff came from. My husband and I were just standing there, afraid to say anything.

She took us through the bedroom, and she had a rope bed that was the bed they slept on. (After we got out of there, my husband said, "How do they sleep on that rough bed when here we're complaining because our mattresses are not comfortable!") Then she took us into the kitchen, and the kitchen was big; had a large fireplace, and had this cabinet with her dishes in it. The table in the middle was hand-made. All this stuff was country-made, except the wicker furniture. In the fireplace she had this swinging thing with a pot on it, and she had a pot of something cooking in the fireplace. I said, "Oh, Mrs. Busbee, that just smells so good." And she says, "Yes, I'm cooking a pot of beans for my weekend guests. I have people that just drop in all the time, and I try to keep a pot of beans going for them."

Then, all of a sudden, she was through with us. She just stood there—she must have been getting a little tired. It seemed sure she was a little bit mentally tired, as it would kind of come and go—but then all of a sudden she said, "Goodbye." So we went on out and went down to the shop.

The famous fireplace at Jugtown with kettle and bean pot on the hearth.

wrote a book and made lectures. I attended one, bought her book and had her autograph it. It was all very interesting. But the school didn't last long.

But then after Vernon started potting, the quality of the pottery got better. I don't remember when Vernon started signing some of his pottery. We would not always buy every time we went down, as we were interested in just seeing what was there and what was being made, but then when Vernon started signing his stuff, I did get several pieces of his that were signed, because I felt it would be more valuable. And one of his pieces I did eventually sell at a nice little profit. As time went along I did sell other pieces, because we did get them for investment and to go along with our social security and retirement.

From the period of about fifty-one to sixty-one, we were going to the Jugtown area at least once a month. That's when we discovered the Moore potters. But we always would go to Jugtown first, and then work back from there. I'll bet you that there weren't many people that bought pottery down there for utility. A lot of people were like we were. We liked it, and we liked to look at and display it, and wash it, and handle it, and put it back, and talk about it.

At one period, while Ben Owen was still potting—this was before Mrs. Busbee had invited us into her house—we asked one of the girls in the shop if we could watch Mr. Owen pot. So she said, "Oh yeah." So we went down, and he was there throwing a pot of some sort. I could tell then that his hands were getting so crippled, and he was aging from the hard work of being a potter. We watched him for a bit. He wasn't very talkative, but we didn't spend too much time then with him. I think we just saw him at Jugtown the one time.

But the first time we went after Mr. Ben had left Jugtown, I distinctly remember looking at the pottery in the shop and it was so thin and didn't seem the same quality that Mr. Ben had been making. I bought a casserole with a lid on it and when we got home my husband said: "What did you buy THAT for?" I said, "I got it to make a comparison between what's being made now and what Ben Owen made." After Mr. Ben left Jugtown and Mrs. Busbee had passed away, the estate was turned over to a management that had Mrs. Sweezy go in and Jugtown was made into a school, or apprentice place, for those who wanted to learn potting. The stuff was potted well and glazed well, but just not the quality as had been. During Mrs. Sweezy's time there, she

After Mr. Owen left Jugtown, one day my husband said, "We ought to find out something about this pottery. I wonder if we could go see Mr. Ben and talk to him." So, I wrote the Owens a letter, and told them that we had this pottery we would like to get identified. And I said, "If Mr. Owen feels like seeing us, we'd like to set up an appointment and come down and see him." Two or three days later we got a letter back from Mrs. Owen saying he would be happy to see us, "but you will have to make an appointment." We found out later that people were just going in to see him without making appointments, and he was in his wheelchair by then. So we had a Saturday morning appointment at eleven o'clock. I got all our pottery together and packed it up, went down there, and went in, and when we walked into their home, here were these shelves on all these walls with all this stuff he had done; real special pieces, and pieces that he had done specially for her or maybe some special occasion like a birthday. I was just drooling all over the place.

That was just an enjoyable day. We got the stuff out and he looked at it. And I said, "This jug, these old pieces, I feel like you potted these." And he says, "Wait a minute, here's a piece that I potted, but I didn't glaze." And I said, "How could you tell that you didn't glaze that?" And he said, "Because Mrs. Busbee would help me sometimes with the glazing, and she'd just throw the stuff on there, and it would run down and wouldn't finish around the bottom or anything." And he said, "I always finished around the bottom."

During early 1988 we went down to Jugtown first, and I noticed that my husband went in and looked around, then on the way home he was coughing and said, "You know, I picked up some of the dust." And I think that that was the last time that he went.

We liked the atmosphere. It seemed to us that the atmosphere would change after we got into Moore County. It would be a restful feeling, just to get down there and go from one place to the other and be leisurely, and see the people that were working, and what they were doing, and the effort they were putting into all this.

Edited by Douglas DeNatale from a transcript of an interview with Mrs. Paul L. Cox, Greensboro, North Carolina, September 24, 1992, by Sally Council.

Joanne Bluethenthal

Joanne Bluethenthal is a noted collector of Jugtown pottery. Her husband's mother, Janet Weil, and grandmother, Gertrude Weil, were important figures in the North Carolina Federation of Women's Clubs.

My mother-in-law, Janet Weil Bluethenthal, was interested in crafts and in 1970 started to develop a collection of North Carolina pottery. She enrolled me as sort of a picker—I would go around to various places and try to find pieces for her. In 1952 I purchased some pieces of Jugtown from Juliana Busbee, which I gave to my mother-in-law. That started a tradition of purchasing Jugtown to give to people for birthdays, anniversaries, and weddings.

For many years I purchased Jugtown ware to use around the house or to give to people. Eventually, I decided that I wanted to bring together a collection of something that was indigenous to this area and spoke of North Carolina in a special kind of way. It occurred to me at that time that maybe collecting early Jugtown would be one of the ways of accomplishing that goal. And so I began my search for Jugtown pottery made between 1926 and 1959 when the Busbees were running Jugtown and Ben Owen was their master potter.

By that time, Juliana Busbee had died. Through Nancy Sweezy, who came to Jugtown in 1968 to follow in the Busbee tradition and keep the pottery going, and some people in Greensboro, I began to find that there were some collections around and auctions here and there where so-called old Jugtown was available. And so I started collecting with the help of Nancy and Vernon Owens, the current owner and master potter of Jugtown since 1962.

During the Busbee era when people went to Jugtown they often took a little brown bag with their lunch in it. Mrs. Busbee liked to have people sit down on her porch for lunch and she sometimes would come out to chat, which was a very pleasant and interesting experience.

Juliana Busbee was very colorful both in personality and dress. She liked earthy tones, oranges and browns, and the

A dome-lidded cracker jar with two different vase forms made at Jugtown ca. late 1940s. The vase on the right, with its controlled drips, exemplified the Busbees' pleasure in creating something that had a hand-made quality to it as opposed to the cold precision of a factory piece.

An "Oriental Jar" in "Mirror Black" glaze with an arrangement of flowers. Juliana Busbee was an expert at creating a mood or a tableau with household objects and native flowers.

colors of wildflowers, and she was inclined to dress accordingly. There were always lovely flowers around, both inside and out. She liked flowers and pieces of cloth that were bright in color.

I think Jugtown pottery is beautiful. The simplicity of it and the fact that the clay came from right in North Carolina made it especially appealing to me. It is of North Carolina and bespeaks of an era that was very charming in many ways.

When you look at the pottery you can tell which pieces the Busbees glazed and which ones Ben Owen glazed, because he was very meticulous about how he did things, therefore, his pieces were nice and even on the bottom. The pieces glazed by Mrs. Busbee would have been sort of uneven because she believed in doing things in the most natural way. She would put the glaze on and let it come down whatever way it happened to come down which resulted in a less clearly defined bottom border than those pieces glazed by Ben Owen.

I visited with Ben Owen several times after I began collecting, but by the time I met him he was so arthritic that he was confined to a wheelchair and was no longer able to pot. His grandson, Ben Owen III, picked up the tradition of pottery making and was fortunate to have learned that art

knee of his grandfather who shared with him all of his knowledge and experience. His grandfather was very proud of the fact that his grandson was going to follow in his tradition—he was really thrilled about it.

Edited by Douglas DeNatale from a transcript of an interview with Joanne Bluethenthal, Greensboro, North Carolina, December 9, 1992, by Douglas DeNatale.

William Moore

A native of Asheboro, North Carolina, William Moore is the director of the Greensboro Historical Museum.

I grew up in Asheboro in the forties and early fifties. My earliest recollection of pottery would be while visiting family and friends' homes where the mantles would often have a pair of the Chinese candlesticks—the famous Jugtown shape—and other pieces around. It was just a part of the family furnishings in the house; pottery had a tradition in the area for many, many years by that time. It was something you noticed because of the unusual glazes and shapes. Later on, I learned that many of the pieces were influenced by Chinese and European designs. The early years of manufacturing do not seem to show a conscious effort by people to collect the pottery for investment as much as a decorative utilitarian form. Of course, that all changed in later decades because of the rarity of the pottery and its appeal to collectors.

Collecting is a very interesting phenomenon. It brings some order to chaos—you're able to bring together something of your own desire and interest, and arrange that in whatever fashion you want. Once you get a certain series of items together that you feel are complete, then you feel uplifted, as if completing a task. You feel as if you have satisfied some particular part of your personality. Pottery collecting has a special appeal to many people. It brings shape, decoration and color to a high level of personal satisfaction.

forms of English and Germanic origins. Jugtown has had a great influence on the other potters of the area, being one of the oldest and one of the most well-established institutions.

I love natural earth colors in glazes, and they seem to appeal to my eye much more than some of the commercial glazes of today. I would like to see Jugtown do more of the traditional forms. When I say traditional, I'm referring to the European, German and adaptive local traditional forms, along with the Chinese forms.

We have all observed early pieces that obviously show that the people making them were creating it strictly for utilitarian purposes and were not concerned as much with artistic form. They might have put some decoration on the surface, or with the glaze, but most pieces were probably not judged for their artistic merit. I think those early potters would have loved to have had people like Vernon Owens working for them. From a historical standpoint,

A series of different bowl forms made at Jugtown holding bulbs. On the back of the photograph Juliana Busbee described these forms and how much each cost left to right: 1. Bulb bowl—mottled blue and red 1.50, 2. Bulb bowl—black .50, 3. Bulb bowl—mottled blue and red 1.25, 4. Bulb bowl—dented—greenish .50.

I think I was in high school the first time I ever went to the potteries, because local history began to intrigue me during this time. I heard people talk about the Busbees, Ben Owen, and other potters of the area.

When I think historically of Jugtown, my impression is that the families represented there over the years were the ones who opened the eyes of many people to the traditional

I would like to see more of these traditional forms revived and kept in production.

Nancy Sweezy did a good job of promoting Jugtown in a scholarly manner when she was the owner. She had a good feeling for the preservation of the Jugtown heritage, and kept the traditional forms alive. She hired local people to help her with that, and I think she maintained the integrity of the site and its products. Her entry to the Jugtown scene was a time for the rediscovery of the arts and crafts of the area. She had a very special talent for sustaining the Jugtown tradition while managing a profitable enterprise. Fortunately, Vernon Owens and his family have continued this tradition by employing excellent potters and delivering high-quality products.

Today, there's so much demand for a high volume of production that the potters of the Seagrove area are not able to spend the time to create all the beautiful pieces I'm sure they are capable of producing. I'm sure it must be frustrating for many of those potters who possess the talent, desire to have their good work recognized, but must produce something less than their talent allows in order to keep up with demand. If they really had their choice, they probably would only produce a few pieces a day, however many their creative talents would allow.

Edited by Douglas DeNatale from a transcript of an interview with William Moore, Greensboro, North Carolina, September 24, 1992, by Sally Council.

Jugtown Pottery Renewed

Seated in the cabin at Jugtown, ca. 1960, are left to right Bob Owens, Charles Moore, and Vernon Owens.

Joe Wilkinson

Joe Wilkinson is an antiques dealer and appraiser in Raleigh, North Carolina, with a strong interest in North Carolina pottery. In the early 1970s he studied pottery as an apprentice to Dorothy Auman, a noted potter and historian of the local pottery tradition of the Seagrove area.

In the late 1960s my parents used to buy a lot of pottery, mostly dinnerware, from Ben Owen, J. B. Cole Pottery and the Aumans. From 1968 through the early 1970s, we would visit them every couple of months and buy a few pieces each time. It was a fun outing, and I took an interest in pottery.

I took a real interest to Dot the first time we met. She said, "If you want to come down in the summer and work with us, you'd be welcome. You'd have to earn your board and keep." So I did.

The summer of 1972 was my first year there. I guess I was a junior in high school. I mowed all the lawns down there, and I did make pottery. This was right after the lead scare, right in the throws of it, matter of fact. I was tested for lead, and I showed up positive. But the people who had worked in the pottery for years, none of them showed up positive. Of course, I had grown up in Raleigh, in the city.

Anyway, this was the time they were developing new glazes without lead. People were real frantic. Dot and Nancy Sweezy were working real close and so were Melvin and Vernon. They were, all four of them, experimenting with different glazes to try to get a non-lead glaze. So there was a lot of travelling back and forth. The Aumans decided they would all work together, and when they got maybe four or five or six good colors that worked, they would sort of divide them up. One would take the green. They were trying to find a green for Dot. Everybody would have their own unique colors.

I don't remember Jugtown producing a whole lot of pottery. Nancy was there, and there were a lot of people coming through in the summer, and they would stay for an internship.

I remember Dot's biggest fear, this was in 1972, was that traditional pottery was dying. Ben Owen had just closed up. When the lead scare came along, he just decided he wasn't going to open again. Of course, the Coles—Waymon was in bad health. For all intents and purposes it looked like traditional North Carolina pottery was going to die in the next two or three years. It looked pretty bad at that time.

Nancy and Vernon were working with trying to get Jugtown really back on track. I hate to use the term counter-culture, but it was people interested in getting closer to the earth and making pottery that basically gave the infusion back into the traditional crafts. I think that the seventies was one of the great transition periods for North Carolina traditional pottery. The torch was passed on to people who had not necessarily grown up in pottery.

Of course, there were some strong family ties, especially Vernon, Melvin, Boyd and all those. The Owen line is very strong. But you'll see a lot of potters have set up down there. There must be twenty or thirty potters around now. They're the off-shoot of the hippy culture that showed an interest in pottery early on. Ultimately, they've played on the traditional aspects of the pottery down there, but they've also introduced things they learned in art school.

Dot didn't talk much about her relationship with the Busbees. She said they used to visit. But Dot was always

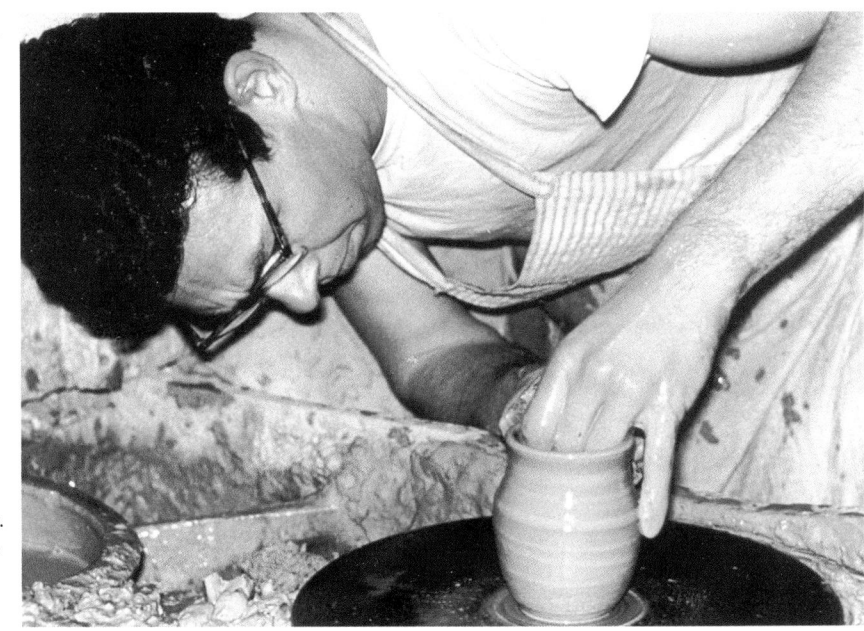

Vernon Owens turning a piece at Jugtown, ca. 1963.

interested in what was purely factual about a piece of pottery. When was it made? Who made it? And Juliana was really more wrapped up in the romanticism of art pottery. If she didn't know something about a piece, she would make it up. That would bother Dot.

Before the Busbees arrived, the Aumans and J. H. Owen were the ones that were going broke making utilitarian pottery, and they turned to art pottery to survive. By 1910, they couldn't make money making whiskey jugs. But Southern Pines was growing by leaps and bounds. People from New York and other urban areas were moving to Southern Pines because of the golf courses. These people were heavily immersed in the arts and crafts. J. H. Owen and Charlie Teague must have been influenced. And Charlie Auman and J. H. Owen started potteries about the same time in 1918, so they must have hooked into the Southern Pines thing too. They would set up at fairs in Southern Pines. In the 1920s the Aumans had a shop in New York, although I think that was more or less organized by Clay Crafters, an outfit in New York that bought wares from the C. R. Auman pottery. Because Clay Crafters put their own stickers on it, you won't ever find a lot of C. R. Auman pottery signed. I don't know when Clay Crafters began, but it was certainly in operation by the late 1920s. When it went out of business in 1936, it took the C. R. Auman pottery with it. In those years, the late 1930s, I think Charlie Auman was very ill or had passed on, and it was being run by Roy and Ray Auman. Floyd Hilton was working there, too. He'd been there in the early thirties, left, and then went back.

Vernon and Pam are pointedly staying immersed in what is purely Piedmont North Carolina traditional pottery, whereas the glitz and the money is in the neo-folk art of the face jugs, which is certainly not a traditional Piedmont Carolina form. They have resisted jumping on the bandwagon. There's a lot of money to be made by making face jugs. Vernon Owens could make a lot of money just by turning out face jugs if he wanted to, and he hasn't. He has tried to preserve what is traditionally Owens, what is traditionally Jugtown, what is traditionally Piedmont North Carolina.

I see other art markets, and I've seen them all crash due to things like the limited editions of face jugs being done. Jugtown has steered clear of that. They have sort of kept the traditions pure and not muddied the water. I respect them a whole lot for that.

Edited by Jane Pryzbysz from a transcript of an interview with Joe Wilkinson, Spring Hope, North Carolina, November 18, 1993, by Jill Severn.

Nancy Sweezy

From 1968 to 1983, Nancy Sweezy directed the Jugtown Pottery for Country Roads, Incorporated. She is also a noted scholar of southeastern pottery. She is the author of Raised in Clay: The Southern Pottery Tradition.

It's awfully hard to analyze what the Busbees were all about having never known them. I think like many people—indeed like myself—they were caught by the charm of the pots and the area. They were both artists—Juliana an illustrator and Jacques a painter. Both were moderately successful but at the same time they had a romantic twinge and shared a yearning for adventure. When they discovered the Seagrove area they saw it as an open door to adventure and they walked through the door.

When they built Jugtown they created an environment that people wanted to be in, wanted to touch and be part of. They made pottery as it was made in the nineteenth century: potters dug clay and ground it in a mule-drawn pug mill; stood on an earth floor to turn the ware on treadle kickwheels; used wood to burn it in groundhog kilns. The buildings were all made of hand-hewn logs, heated by fireplaces, decorated with homespun weavings and furnished with chairs and tables made locally. This deliberately created a romantic environment that was enticing. Everybody knew it wasn't quite real, but they could pretend it was the old way. But gracious old, not old with problems or difficulties.

There was a certain magic that Mrs. Busbee was in charge of. She fostered an image, created a special ambience at Jugtown. She was a social person and encouraged her city friends to visit her whenever they could. She always cooked meals for her guests in the open fireplace of the dining room. And, afterwards, she washed the dishes in a gorgeous, big, Chinese blue glazed bowl. All this fostered the mystique of a life lived in an older style. But hidden behind a curtain there was a tiny modern kitchen with a stove and a sink. The bathroom had modern plumbing and you would find there books written in French or German and magazines from all over the world. Very sophisticated stuff, you know, strange to find in Seagrove, North Carolina.

The Busbees were part of the arts and crafts movement, much in vogue then in England and America, which rose in defiance of the impersonalness and conformity of manufactured products. As people who were living out the beliefs of this movement, they acquired a terrific reputation and following among the savants and elite of North Carolina; it became a very "in" thing to know about, to buy and use Jugtown ware, and especially to be numbered among the Busbees' friends.

The rhetoric was that they were "saving the tradition"—pretty flowery rhetoric by our standards. But certainly they did want to see the local pottery making continue, and this goal completely tied in with what they sought to do with their own lives. Perhaps they thought if they made this type of pottery others would continue to make it too. And, further, if they made it to a "higher" standard (which was really a different standard), it would elevate everybody's work. Benevolence was viewed as a high moral value at that time.

The Busbees had a considerable effect on the marketing of North Carolina pottery. The whole economy was changing, and as it changed, there was less and less need for the old-type utilitarian pots. So, the community's potteries were either changing or going out of business. That process had begun by the time that the Busbees came on the scene during the World War I years. It's very hard to weed out just what the influence of Jugtown was. It certainly had an influence. But you know how stubborn the potters are—they're going to be very aware of what's happening at the new pottery, they're going to pick it all up, but they're not going to look directly at it. Jugtown was in some ways an irritant. But, to think that these potters would change their ways because of Jugtown probably would not be correct. What did affect them very much was the fact that Juliana Busbee was an enormously successful promoter and brought people and news coverage into the area. Juliana really helped put Seagrove on the map.

It was Jacques's ideas and vision around which Jugtown ware developed. He was never a potter himself, so I had a hard time figuring out how this relationship between him and Ben Owen could work as well as it apparently did. He had in his mind what the shapes ought to look like. Jacques was a scholar. He studied pottery made in other times and parts of the world -- especially China -- in museums and books. He said to himself, "I don't want just any old pot. I want it to have this graceful, slow... coming from a nice foot, to a big belly, to a shoulder... and the shoulder can't be down here, it's got to be up here... and the neck and lip must be strong." He had as a goal an abstract perfection of form which the local potters had never had. That wasn't their goal. They made some perfectly wonderful forms, but they weren't looking at them and saying, "It's perfect, it's not perfect." But he was.

Ben Owen's own innate abilities, combined with Busbee's influence made Ben truly a master of classical pottery form. And his grandson, Ben Owen III, has picked that up and will be a fine potter, too. You have to give care and attention to form, which is the essence of pottery. You have to glaze and fire properly, but if you haven't got the form right, then forget it.

Nancy Sweezy and Vernon Owens in the turning room at Jugtown, ca. 1971. "Vernon and I had to develop a system of working together which we did very amenably for a long time," recalls Nancy Sweezy.

from the South, Norman would weave in the shop, and I would work with them to make it an educational operation as well as a shop. And we did this. The store was incredible. You could learn about the craftspeople, how they wove baskets or carved toys, and also buy their handwork and take it home.

When Ralph went to the Smithsonian, I was, by then, totally hooked on these lively folk arts and artists. I had been a potter for years, but had known nothing of traditional southern pottery. I made two long trips through Appalachia to meet the people whose work I'd been promoting and talking about in Cambridge. It was a mind-opening experience to be totally welcomed by these artisans, to see their work and processes and lives. Ralph kept saying, "You've got to visit the potteries—you're a potter." So, we came out of the mountains into the Piedmont at the end of the second trip and went to see the potteries. I'll never forget driving into Jugtown, coming into those trees, and looking around at the log cabins in the trees—the way anybody can today—and just being jolted by the sense of magic in this enclave.

If you look at what happened at Jugtown with a sense of justice, Ben Owen, by all rights, should have inherited that pottery. I don't doubt that at all. But, it just didn't happen that way. The Busbees did not make his future secure there. Mrs. Busbee died in 1962 and so did John Maré, who owned the pottery at that time. When Country Roads bought Jugtown in 1968 and I went there to live and work, this whole contentious business (although long since legally settled) was alive and well in people's minds. I know, because I fell into it—wham. It was a strange thing to come into after all those years. After all, Ben Owen had left Jugtown to open his pottery in 1959. In my early days there a lot of people told me quite frankly that the place ought to be closed, because anybody else—meaning me, of course—would tamper with and spoil it. And we did tamper with it. If we hadn't, it wouldn't exist today.

Before all this, Country Roads' first venture was with a craft store in Cambridge, Massachusetts. Ralph Rinzler, Norman Kennedy and I organized it so people in the Boston area could know of the handcrafts of Appalachia. Ralph was finding them when he went down through the mountains looking for musicians to bring to the Newport Folk Festival. When he found a fiddler, he often would also find a quilter or woodcarver. And those people were having a hard time selling crafts. They needed more income and their work, unique and humorous, was well worth supporting.

I had injured my back and was unable to make pots at that time, so Ralph approached me and Norman about starting a craft shop. The plan was that he would bring the work up

Vernon Owens was sitting in the sales cabin, as glum a young man on that day as I have ever seen. I looked at the few pots in the shop and then asked Vernon if I could see the house. He said, "Well, I don't know, why do you want to do that?" I said, "I just want to do it." So, he opened the door of the log cabin that had been the Busbee home. I walked through it, sat in it and began to mull on my almost visceral response to this place. By the time we left, I was thinking that I'd talk to Ralph about Country Roads buying the pottery. If we could raise the funds I would live and work there. It happened just like that. Yes, it was something like a conversion experience. Jugtown obviously played on some need in me. That visit was in June and by the end of August, Country Roads had bought the place and I had moved there. My children were with me there at various times; two of them and a number of their friends came with me at the beginning to help rebuild the kilns and daub the log house. This was the late 1960s, remember, and counter-culture was well under way in the North but had not yet hit the South. Seagrove had never seen anything like these young people and I'm afraid we were pretty much of a shock.

We had apprentices from the very beginning—that was part of the deal. Country Roads wanted to put the pottery back on its feet for sure, but we also wanted young people to learn how to make pottery this way. We had wanted to involve more local people in the program than we were able to, but at least we were teaching. We quickly realized that having apprentices for six weeks over the summer wasn't enough, so we made the program flexible and had people staying a year, two, sometimes three years, really learning a lot. If you learn to make pots in a working pottery you learn the whole process—from digging and processing clay, through turning, glazing, burning and selling. You need to know about all these things to run your own shop. Some very fine potters, who have their own shops now, came out of it and we are very proud of them.

How can we compare my work at Jugtown to the Busbees? When the Busbees and Ben Owen worked together it was a different era. Then (and as a man) Jacques Busbee could direct Ben's work in a way that would not have been acceptable to Vernon or for that matter, to me. The legend is that—at least in the early years—Busbee would knock some of Ben's pots off the long boards with his cane, saying, "That one and that one won't do." Now, I'll tell you, that is not the kind of thing you could have done to Vernon when I went to Jugtown. It would have been all over in a second. But Ben... those were hard times and Ben was a young man and he was apparently able to put up with it. When I was there we had a partnership, not an employer-employee relationship. But, of course, I had some goals I wanted to work toward. I wanted the shapes we made to

Did I go to Jugtown with a sense of mission? That's hard to analyze. Yes and no. We knew that the other buyers looking at the pottery would have closed it down and used the property for other purposes, so we felt that Country Roads was the right buyer. I'm a potter and would go there to help preserve it. I didn't go there thinking I knew more than the Jugtown potters knew; I went there to work with Vernon and Bob and Charles in a collaboration. However, I did know some technical things that had to be done, especially about glazes and marketing. I knew that they shouldn't be working constantly with raw red lead glaze. It was dangerous and I knew the shop would be closed for using it. So, while it was clear I could personally make a contribution, the real mission was for all of us together to make this unique pottery viable again. If Country Roads had not bought the pottery it is questionable whether it would exist today.

Bob Owens loads a ground-hog kiln at Jugtown, ca. 1971

We made the change to safer, fritted lead glazes and then to higher temperature glazes not requiring lead to melt them. This change disturbed many customers, even outraged some, who had been buying the old, soft, very beautiful, red lead glaze ware. One man shook his fist in my face and said, "Damn you! What are you doing to this place? We can't get the old orange anymore." I worked on the glazes, Vernon worked on the kilns, and we all worked on the clay bodies and firing problems. We changed a lot of things together. In a sense, I was helping the Jugtown potters (and occasionally some of the others) through a period of transition by adding my skills and knowledge to theirs.

be full-bodied, strong, and spontaneous; I wanted the new glazes to be rich in color and brought to life by fire. I hoped we could diminish production losses and build up a pleased clientele. And, as a team, we more or less did this.

Strangely, many potters don't discipline themselves to "see" form. For me, pottery is form. The glaze has to be appropriate for the shape and the pot has to be fired right. But first, it is an art involving form. The traditional potters in the South were concerned primarily with the utility of their shapes and not their aesthetic qualities. It's a very self-conscious and sophisticated thing to look at a pot, examine and assess it, but that's what Busbee did and it was my natural inclination to do this also.

When Vernon came into Jugtown as a young man of seventeen or eighteen to be the Jugtown potter, he tried for a little while to make pots just the way Ben had made them. He decided very quickly that this was not natural to him and that he had to be his own man. He struggled with his

Apprentice pieces made at Jugtown during the Country Roads era, 1968-1983. From left to right: Small bundt pan in "Wood Smoke" glaze by Agnes Chabot, 1973; "Spoon Jar" in white glaze by Cynthia Burns, 1980; Collander in brown feldspathic glaze by Pamela Lorette, 1981. All from the collection of Pamela and Vernon Owens.

own style, which was very clutched up and tense at first, and gradually loosened and opened up.

Vernon and I had to develop a system of working together which we did very amenably for a long time. I had a lot to learn from him and from Bobby and I guess I was able to convey this because they didn't take umbrage when I thought they had something to learn from me. Now and then, Vernon and I would look at a board of pots he'd just turned; the shapes were near alike, but one or two would stand out as especially good examples. We'd try to figure out why, and this led us into careful thinking about form and most times we would see it in the same way. Through interaction like this, we each became more aware of what we were striving towards and his eye became more and more keen as he matured into a master potter.

Seagrove is quite a different place today. I find the build-up of potteries in the area strange. Some have a family or other connection with traditional pottery making, but most are simply coming to the area because it's a good marketing place. It's okay. It makes things livelier and it's not harming the older potteries to have all these newcomers. I'm hoping the proposed pottery museum will be established in Seagrove because I think the public can find out more about the evolution and techniques of pottery making here. If you bring in exhibits and materials and scholarships so people can learn more about pottery, it will increase their understanding and interest and the potters will find it useful, too. I think the next step is to get this museum built. Its programs and galleries will raise pottery making to a higher level. The commerce will continue, but we can also celebrate the potters and recognize pottery making as the art form it is.

At the end we come to the question: what about the future? You can't create any more traditional potters like Burlon Craig and Lanier Meaders. They came out of a certain time period, and you're not going to have them again. There are going to be younger people who have learned from them, but the lifestyle of today is different and today's potters will do what potters have always done—they'll make every effort they can to make a good living. This means making some changes in a changing world. But not changes that cater to the lowest popular tastes. You don't attain stature that way. But you can be a potter with high standards and be successful as well. However, things don't go on now as they did in the past—to think that the lifeways of an earlier era can be recaptured involves a nostalgia which becomes artificial after a while. The work has to come out of the real life of today. We just have to put a good quality edge on today's work and keep it there.

Edited by Douglas DeNatale from transcripts of interviews with Nancy Sweezy, Jacksonville, Florida, October 18, 1992 and Robbins, North Carolina, December 8, 1992, by Douglas DeNatale.

Earthenware

number	name	size (w x h)	shipping weight (lbs)	price
	bowls			
11	soup bowl with handles	5½ x 2	1½	2.50
12a	soup bowl without handles	6 x 2¼	1½	2.25
12b	serving bowl	9 x 3½	3½	4.50
13a	salad bowl	5½ x 1¾	1½	2.00
13b	salad serving bowl	8½ x 2½	3½	4.50
14	flared bowl	11 x 4	5	5.50
15	punch or large salad bowl	10½ x 7½	7½	10.00
	pitchers, tea, coffee			
30b	pitcher, small	1½ pint	2	3.50
30c	pitcher, medium	1½ quart	3½	5.00
30d	pitcher, large	2½ quart	5	6.50
31a	flared rim pitcher, tiny	¾ pint	1½	2.50
31b	flared rim pitcher, small	1½ pint	2½	3.50
36	teapot	5 cups	4½	10.00
37a	cream pitcher	4 x 3	1	2.50
37b	sugar bowl	3 x 3½	2	2.50
38	coffee pot	6½ x 8½	5	8.50
	casseroles and beanpots			
40a	Coolie top casserole, sm.	1 pint	2½	3.75
40b	Coolie top casserole, lg.	2 quart	7	8.50
41	flat top casserole, medium	1½ quart	5	5.75
42	round casserole, large	2 quart	6½	8.00
45a	beanpot, small	1½ quart	3	3.75
45b	beanpot, medium	2 quart	4½	5.25
45c	beanpot, large	3 quart	6½	7.25
	pie and baking dishes			
50	Jugtown pie	9½ x 2	4	3.75
51a	fluted pie	10 x 2	4	3.75
51b	fluted bake, large	11½ x 3½	5	6.50
52	chicken pie	10 x 3	4	5.00
53a	ring bake, medium	9 x 2	4	5.00
53b	ring bake, large	11½ x 2¼	7½	10.00
	plates and platters			
71a	Jugtown saucer	6	1	1.50
71b	Jugtown lunch plate	8	2½	2.50
71c	Jugtown dinner plate	10½	3½	4.00
72a	bent plate, tiny	6	1½	1.75
72b	bent plate, small	8	2½	2.75
72c	bent plate, medium	10½	3½	4.00
72d	bent plate, large	12	6	7.50
73	ring platter, large	14	7	10.00
74a	Jugtown II, saucer	6	1	1.50
74b	Jugtown II, lunch plate	8	2½	2.50
74c	Jugtown II, dinner plate	10½	3½	4.00
	cups and mugs			
80	noggin	3 x 3¼	1	1.25
81a	noggin with handle, small	3 x 3	1	1.75
81b	noggin with handle, large	3½ x 3¾	1½	2.50
82	Confederate cup	3¾ x 3	1½	2.00
83	straight mug	3¼ x 4	1½	2.25
84	wine cup	2½ x 3	1	1.25
85	Jugtown teacup	3½ x 2½	1	1.50
86	Jugtown II, teacup	3½ x 2¾	1	1.50
	miscellaneous			
90a	candlesticks, small	8	5	6.50 pr.
90b	candlesticks, large	12	10	10.00 pr.
91	candlesaucer	6	2	3.00
92	egg cup	3 x 3	½	1.25
93	beehive bank	4 x 5½	2	2.50
95a	birdhouse, unglazed, small	5½ x 7	3	2.50
95b	birdhouse, unglazed, large	6½ x 8½	4½	3.50
96a	birdhouse, glazed, small	5½ x 7	3	3.25
96b	birdhouse, glazed, large	6½ x 8½	4½	4.50

Stoneware

number	name	size (w x h)	shipping weight (lbs)	price stoneware	price salt
	bowls				
101	tiny	4½ x 2	1½	2.50	
102a	fluted, tiny	4½ x 2½	1	2.50	
102b	fluted, small	6 x 2½	2	3.00	
102c	fluted, medium	7½ x 4½	4	5.00	
102d	fluted, large	9 x 5½	6	7.00	
103a	thumbprint, medium	6½ x 4½	3½	5.00	
103b	thumbprint, large	7½ x 5	4½	7.00	
104	plain	7 x 4	3½	5.00	5.50
105a	angular, tiny	4½ x 2½	1½	2.25	2.50
105b	angular, small	5½ x 3½	2	3.00	3.50
105c	angular, large	9 x 5	5½	7.00	7.50
106	punch	12 x 6½	10	15.00	18.00
107	plain, large (not shown)	9 x 4½	5½	7.00	7.50
	vases				
120	tiny	3 x 5	1½	2.50	2.75
121a	neck vase, tiny	2½ x 3½	1	1.75	2.00
121b	neck vase, small	4 x 6	2	3.00	3.50
121c	neck vase, medium	5½ x 8	3½	5.00	5.50
121d	neck vase, large	7 x 10½	6	8.00	9.00
122a	low, wide vase, small	5 x 4½	2½	3.50	3.75
122b	low, wide vase, large	6½ x 5½	4	5.50	6.00
123a	dragonhead, medium	4½ x 8	3½	5.00	
123b	dragonhead, large	5 x 10½	6	8.00	
124	plain, round	6 x 6½	4	5.00	5.50
125	tapering	5½ x 6½	3½	5.00	5.50
126a	2-handle vase, medium	6 x 8	3½	6.00	6.50
126b	2-handle vase, large	5½ x 10½	8½	9.00	10.00
127	oval	6 x 9½	6	8.00	9.00
128	4-handle vase	5 x 8	4	5.50	6.00
129a	round dragonhead, small	3½ x 4	2	3.00	3.50
129b	round dragonhead, medium	5 x 6½	3½	5.00	5.50
	pitchers				
130a	pitcher, tiny	1¼ cup	1½	2.50	2.75
130b	pitcher, small	2½ cup	2	3.75	4.25
130c	pitcher, medium	1¾ quart	4	5.25	6.00
130d	pitcher, large	2½ quart	5½	7.00	7.50
130e	pitcher, extra large	¾ quart	8½	9.25	10.50
131a	flared rim pitcher, tiny	1 cup	1½	2.50	2.75
131b	flared rim pitcher, small	2 cup	2	3.75	4.25
137a	cream pitcher	1¼ cup	1½	2.75	3.00
137b	sugar bowl	3 x 3½	2	2.75	3.00
	jars				
161	cookie jar	7 x 9½	7½	9.25	10.50
162a	medicine jar, tiny	3½ x 5½	2½	3.75	4.25
162b	medicine jar, small	4½ x 7½	4	5.00	5.50
162c	medicine jar, medium	5 x 8½	5½	6.25	6.75
162d	medicine jar, large	5½ x 10	6½	7.50	8.00
	jugs				
165a	Jugtown jug, small	4½ x 5½	2	3.50	3.75
165b	Jugtown jug, large	7 x 9	6	8.50	9.00
166a	straight jug, tiny	3½ x 5½	2	3.50	3.75
166b	straight jug, small	4 x 8½	3½	5.00	5.75
166c	straight jug, medium	5 x 10	6	7.25	8.00
166d	straight jug, large	6 x 11½	9	9.00	10.00
167a	wine jug, small	5½ x 6½	4	6.00	6.50
167b	wine jug, large	7 x 9	6½	8.50	9.00
	cups and mugs and candlesticks				
180	noggin	3 x 3¼	1	1.50	2.00
181a	noggin with handle, small	3 x 3	1	1.75	2.25
181b	noggin with handle, large	3½ x 3¾	1½	2.50	3.00
182	Confederate cup	3¾ x 3	1½	2.00	2.75
183	straight mug	3¼ x 4	1½	2.00	2.75
184	wine cup	2½ x 3	1	1.25	1.75
190a	candlesticks, small	8	6	6.75 pr.	8.00 pr.
190b	candlesticks, large	12	11	12.00 pr.	14.00 pr.

Price sheet for Jugtown Pottery, 1973. From the collection of Joanne Bluethenthal.

The Legacy of Jugtown

═══ POTTERIES OF THE SEAGROVE AREA ═══

1. New Salem Pottery
2. E. J. King Pottery
3. Earth Spirit Pottery
4. Latham Pottery
5. Beaumont Pottery
6. Raven Pottery
7. Fat Beagle Pottery
8. Turn & Burn Pottery
9. King's Pottery
10. Pottery Junction
11. Dirtworks Pottery
12. Museum Office
13. Old Gap Pottery
14. Phil Morgan Pottery
15. Holly Hill Pottery
16. Whynot Pottery
17. Backwoods Pottery
18. Kovak Pottery
19. Tom Gray Pottery
20. Potts Town Pottery
21. Fork Creek Mill Pottery
22. LDDK Pottery
23. Oakland Pottery
24. R & L Pottery
25. Albright Pottery
26. Dixieland Pottery
27. Wild Rose Pottery
28. Anita Morgan Pottery
29. Shelton's Pottery
30. J. B. Cole Pottery
31. King Road Pottery
32. Cross Creek Pottery

33. Graham Chrisco Pottery
34. Luck's Ware
35. Cagle Road Pottery
36. Olive Branch Pottery
37. Chrisco's Pottery
38. Walton's Pottery
39. Bear Creek Pottery
40. Dover Pottery
41. Rockhouse Pottery
42. Pot Luck Pottery
43. A Teague Pottery
44. Old House Pottery
45. Humble Mill Pottery
46. Ben Owen Pottery
47. Westmoore Pottery
48. My House Pottery
49. O'Quinn Pottery
50. M. L. Owens Pottery
51. Jugtown Pottery
52. Southern Folk Pottery
53. Cady Clay Works
54. Hickory Hill Pottery
55. Down To Earth Pottery
56. Teague's Frogtown Pottery
57. Freeman's Pottery
58. Cagle Pottery
59. Simpatico Pottery
60. Cole's Pottery
61. North Cole Pottery
62. Shovelin' Barefoot Pottery
63. G. F. Cole Pottery

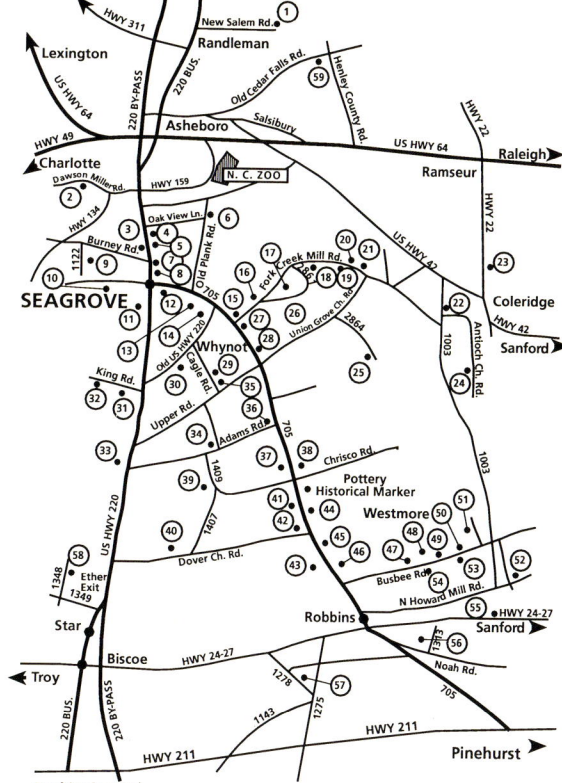

1993 map of Seagrove area showing many of the 63 potteries now located in this area. Printed as part of the Pottery Shop Guide For Seagrove Area compiled by William W. Ivey for the Friends of the N. C. Pottery Museum.

Leonidas J. Betts

Leonidas J. Betts, Department of English, North Carolina State University, Raleigh, North Carolina. In 1993 he was appointed Curator of Ceramics for the North Carolina State University Visual Arts Center, where he is currently curating the exhibition, "Burlon Craig: An Open Window into the Past."

Jugtown is an important part of the arts and craft movement in the twentieth century. It has great significance because it utilized a moribund technology that it somehow miraculously rescued and then wonderfully integrated with an oriental aesthetic. It was a stroke of genius for Jacques Busbee to be able to say, "There is a curious affinity between this local craft and these early Chinese pieces which depend primarily on form rather than on decoration." He would take a shape and not slavishly have it copied in Moore County but he would have it translated in Moore County. If you look at the palette of old Jugtown, it's very limited, and the shapes are very limited, but by using those simple glaze colors, Jugtown produced very elegant work.

It must have been a painful process if Jacques Busbee said to Ben Owen, "Alright. Here it is; make something like this," and then said, "No, the neck is too long, so start again and do another one." It must have been very painful. I always have the sense that Ben Owen didn't get as much credit from the Busbees as he deserved.

There is a lingering controversy over Jugtown's role in keeping the pottery tradition alive. I remember that Dorothy Auman always thought that it really was Pinehurst and Southern Pines and the interest of tourists coming from the outside that were of primary importance. She may have been right to a degree, but you can't overlook the fact that the Busbees were gifted promoters of pottery on a national level, rather than on just a local, tourist level. They must be given credit for making the pottery tradition well-known across the nation and for maintaining certain kinds of pure standards, which made them not always favorably received in the neighborhood, where people were taking other routes.

I've heard older residents of the community speak rather disparagingly of the Busbees as not ever quite assimilating themselves into the life of the community, always somehow being apart from the community. And, of course, I can see the other side of that: it may have been that the locals shunned them, rather than their shunning the locals. I think it may very well have worked both ways. But I don't believe they were warmly received. And I think part of that situation was their self-promotion and their attempt to elevate making pots into something artistic, and perhaps even noble.

I'm not always sure that the Busbees' stories were exactly accurate, because both claimed in one place or another to have discovered the orange pie plate where it all started. But I don't quarrel with their stories. If you're promoting something like a pottery, if it's struggling, or if you're trying to make people aware, you obviously want to play up the quaint and curious elements, whether you have to make them up or whether they really exist.

There was a kind of wonderful collaboration between the Busbees and the patrons who were reporting on what was going on at the pottery. And I think these people frequently were looking for something fabulous. I know a number of people who did go to old Jugtown, and they all have remarkably similar stories. Almost everyone I know who went to Jugtown has a story about being asked to stay for dinner, and having rabbit stew from the fireplace, and being served white liquor from a local moonshiner. If Juliana entertained so many people, the Busbee dining room must have been like Grand Central Station—people coming and going. It's the very favorite story: being one of those favored people allowed to have a meal with the Busbees. It was, to them, like having a meal at the White House.

I think the Busbees cultivated their curious qualities. She's legendary for things like wading out into the muddy field to pick wildflowers on the way to the Governor's Mansion, and wearing her dress inside out at some grand reception. You often wonder how much is genuine and how much is a part of the persona she wished to project. I think one clear evidence of the Busbees' view of themselves is the fact that they changed their names. "Juliana" is much more charming and elegant than Julia and "Jacques" is a bit better than Jack. I think that change really is a paradigm for their view of themselves.

They didn't become countrified. For example, she wore homespun clothing, but I think it was quite consistent with their philosophy of using local materials for artistic purposes. No, I am quite sure that she never was anything but a Raleigh woman of substantial background. It was like the Raj: you go to India and it's awful, but now you have this little outpost of progress where somehow you're utilizing the best of the material from the countryside to produce something that is beautiful.

I think that the Busbees' early devotion to quality and to the aesthetic rather than the simple attractiveness of tourist goods is something that Jugtown still carries on. Jugtown maintains a very high standard of work, and always has. In fact, the pottery becomes increasingly refined and good. That's been one of my themes about Jugtown. There is

Pottery from the collection of Leonidas J. Betts [left to right] Stoneware "Persian Jar" in "Chinese Blue" glaze, by Ben Owen III; Miniature jug in salt-glazed stoneware by Pamela Owens; Churn in salt-glazed stoneware by Vernon Owens.

continuing movement and a growth in the pottery, rather than stagnation. Whenever Jugtown has come within a breath of vanishing from the face of the earth, almost miraculously somebody has stepped in and has saved it and has kept it going and has made an enormous contribution to the place. There's a continuing prejudice about classic Jugtown: if it's not old Jugtown, it's not Jugtown. Personally, I'm looking for grace—not the fact that it's old Jugtown with that burden of history that it carries. Mere age is not very important to me. There is at Jugtown always the potential for surprise and improvement and re-definition and progress.

Vernon was a kid of eighteen when he came to work for John Maré. Maré clearly wanted to preserve the sense of old Jugtown. Vernon began by making slavish copies of old Jugtown, and sometimes not entirely successfully. He tried to copy broken pieces that he found around the pottery, which were probably discarded because they weren't good examples. So early on he abandoned that copyist mode and began to try to make what he felt was a good shape. I look at the Maré catalog, and then I look at Jugtown under Nancy Sweezy, and Vernon's shapes have become more

graceful, but still too clearly tied to the early Jugtown aesthetic. I think it's only when Vernon began to sense that he was going to be truly the master at Jugtown that he began experimenting in a serious way with his forms.

Vernon has made his pottery more and more and more artistic, but without talking about it, without making it a matter of public concern. If you call Vernon an artist, he becomes very nervous, because that's not what he sees himself as. He makes pots, he says. Vernon and Pam are prospering because they are constantly improving and innovating. I hope that history is going to record how vitally important Pam has been in the operation. She's very much an intellectual, and she's very much a person who's always looking for a way to improve things. She's the one who is doing the glaze chemistry and experimenting. I think it's amazing that you have two people who have this remarkable collaboration.

I see a parallel between Ben Owen III and Vernon. I think that people will look at a work by Ben and say, "Oh, yes. That's Ben III." They won't think: "Well, that may be Ben Owen III copying Ben Owen. I've got to turn up the item and see what's written on the bottom to tell which it is."

Ben has seen a larger world. He's had a classical ceramic education at East Carolina University and he's been exposed to a whole different way of perceiving things. But I don't think his education is going to spoil him. He will simply use his education to grow as an artist.

I know there always has been a Jugtown mystique. I get a kind of chill every time I walk onto the property. I think about Juliana's ashes scattered there under the pine trees. I remember reading the newspaper account that as she was being scattered there was a snow that dusted the quince blooming in the compound. You know—that does something.

The mystique has continued, and it's mysterious even though I've never seen Pam and Vernon do anything in terms of promotion comparable to what the Busbees did. Still, it's there, the mystery is there. It's that basic mystery that all good pottery has, because it's the elements: it's earth and air and fire and water, and that's all it is. Somehow it's so elemental that it becomes almost holy.

I'm rather saddened by the staggering increase in pottery establishments in the Moore County area because they dilute the possibility of customers going down and understanding what has happened historically. Making pots is such a wonderful North Carolina tradition, and I hope the tradition won't be diluted. I am not saying that I hope these new people don't sell their pots, but I truly want people to understand the meaning of certain kinds of pots, that they are the evolutionary end of a magical process that's been going on for two hundred years.

Edited by Douglas DeNatale from a transcript of an interview with Leonidas Betts, Fuquay-Varina, North Carolina, December 8, 1992, by Douglas DeNatale.

Ben Owen III

Ben Owen III is the grandson of Ben Owen. He began turning pottery at the age of nine, under the tutelage of his grandfather. He recently completed his M.F.A. in ceramics from East Carolina University.

When I was growing up, my grandfather was my companion and care-giver after school. I'd get out of school and go next door to where my grandfather lived, and sit on the porch with him. I'd just pass the afternoon talking, listening and learning from whatever he talked about.

I grew up around the pots and things he made that were in our house, and I was always fascinated by them. Sometimes you take things for granted because they are around you all the time, but to other people they're very special because they did not grow up with them. But as time went along and I got older, my grandfather would take me out to the shop and show me what he used to do. He wasn't able to work on the wheel anymore since he'd retired in 1972 because of arthritis and poor health. I was about four years old then. But when I was eight or nine, he would show me how he used to work on the wheel.

least several times a week. I couldn't wait to get out of school because I was going to go home and have some fun. And what better person to have it with? I really became fascinated with making clay and it was a challenge to me to try to make some of the shapes and forms my grandfather had on the shelf in the house. He always told me, "You always try to make the hardest shape there is possible." I made my first candle holder when I was about eleven or twelve years old. You know, I was trying to make the hardest thing, what my grandfather considered the hardest thing. He wanted me to work on the basic things. I would make coffee mugs or bowls and things like that. But I really like the

Ben Owen, grandfather of Ben Owen III, turns a "Korean Bowl" at his Old Plank Road Pottery, ca. 1960s. "My grandfather's philosophy was that simplicity in form and shape was the key. It is easy to be complicated, but hard to keep things simple. This is kind of my philosophy, too," explains Ben Owen III.

Nothing had been touched since everything was shut down in 1972. There was still clay sitting over in one corner of the room. The wheel was still sitting there. The ware boards were empty, except for some green ware pots he never finished firing. He would show me how to wet down the clay. The clay was dried out, and he showed me how to wet it back down, and then let it dry in the sun. Then we would get some clay ready, and he'd get on the wheel or he'd get me on the wheel, and tell me what I needed to do. He guided me about what I was doing right and what I was doing wrong. He was a great teacher. And we did that at

challenge of moving on to more complicated things. And even though those candlesticks were heavy bottomed or distorted, I was determined to do them. Having my grandfather as a teacher at an early age like that, I kind of began potting like learning to ride a bicycle. I started doing it, and I could stop any time, and then go back to it. I might have been a little "rusty," but it was a lot of fun.

When I was thirteen, my father saw that I had an interest in working in clay, and he decided he would like to open up the shop again. He hoped that maybe one day I would

Ben Owen III turns pottery at his wheel, 1994.

ods. My grandfather studied the shapes and forms of oriental masters, and that was where he got a lot of ideas. He went up North with Mr. Busbee to different museums, and they would sketch out shapes and forms they wanted to recreate in their own translations. It was like me going off to school and getting a degree in fine arts. Learning to explore, change, and grow in your work is important to being not just a craftsman, but an artist. My grandfather grew up and learned to make pots from his father and his grandfather, but he was willing to change and grow and develop.

After I graduated high school, I went to college. I had a fellowship to teach a ceramics class at Pfeiffer

eventually be able to make many pots for the shop. So we hired a potter to work for us, to make things to stock the shop. When I had time after school, I'd make pots. Dad took care of the business part of the pottery, as well as doing the glazing and firing the kiln. He let me stay on the wheel.

When we opened the pottery shop in the early 1980s, there were probably nine or ten pottery shops in the area. Now there's over sixty. A lot of things have happened in the past fifteen years. The local community colleges in the area—Montgomery, Sandhill and Randolph Community Colleges—started offering more classes in pottery. A lot of people saw that people who came to this part of North Carolina were interested in pottery, so they went to school and learned how to make pots. Eventually they moved here and opened up a shop. Some are from families of potters. Like Sid Luck who is a fifth generation potter. He was an educator, but he then became interested in working in clay and wanted to do what his forefathers did. So he's opened up a shop of his own. Others have gone to school and come to this area from out-of-state because they see there's a demand for pottery here. And the more shops in the area, the more people come through. It seems like all of them are doing fine. You know, there are different types of work—anything from very low-priced functional ware to very expensive decorative-type pots.

When my grandfather passed away in October of 1983, I was fifteen years old, but I had learned a lot from him growing up in that environment. I was well on my way. From what he taught me, I was able to think about what to do next, and to look at shapes and forms from other historical peri-

College. I was studying business thinking I could use it to run the pottery one day when I returned home. I taught the class and had a lot of fun with it. I found I was able to teach things that I kind of took for granted. It made me think about what I was doing, how I operated in clay, and what I would do in my life working with clay. Thinking about that I decided, after two years at Pfeiffer, I wanted to go to art school. I did research to find out available schools with strong programs, but not too far away from home. I wanted to be able to come home and make pots, or set up a studio wherever I was, make pots and take them home to have at least a few things in the shop when customers came by.

So I decided to complete my education at East Carolina University. It would have been very easy to stay home and make pots, and I could probably be making a good living right now if I didn't go to school. But at the same time, I didn't think I'd be as well developed. Going to school, or just getting away from the environment you're in, that you take for granted, you're able to reflect back on it. Being at school opened up so many doors. You're able to be in contact with so many different influences, so many different media. You're able to be around other artists, all looking to create their own style.

I did much research in creating new shapes and forms. A lot of shapes and forms that I made were those my grandfather made. And I was just recreating some of the things that he translated. So I've looked harder at the roots and the foundation of my grandfather's style. And I've been creating my own roots, searching for more information so that I can create my own style that relates to something in my family, but at the same time generates something new too.

My grandfather's philosophy was that simplicity in form and shape was the key. It is easy to be complicated, but hard to keep things simple. This is kind of my philosophy, too.

My grandfather was one of the main influences in my life, but I'm also really glad I went to college. While I was at school I came to understand that a potter can learn in two different ways. You learn things being an apprentice like I did working with my grandfather. And you learn things from going outside your environment. You can grasp things there and then bring ideas back. That's what I'm trying to do.

Edited by Jane Przybysz from a transcript of an interview with Ben Owen, Seagrove, North Carolina, January 10, 1994, by Douglas DeNatale.

Pamela Owens

Pam Owens came to Jugtown Pottery in 1977 as a participant in Country Roads' apprenticeship program. She married Vernon Owens in 1983. Today, she and Vernon run Jugtown Pottery.

I was here in 1977. Sherry Erickson, a woman from the school that I went to, heard about Jugtown, and she came back and told them at the school that she wanted to apprentice at Jugtown. She wrote, and the word came back from Nancy Sweezy that Nancy had been neighbors with our pottery teacher, Isobel Karl. So Sherry did come down here, and she was the first of six or seven people that came from that school.

I came as an apprentice in 1977. It was really nice to work somewhere where people were just making pottery and getting it out. My pottery teacher, Mrs. Karl, made it very clear that it would take a long time to learn to make pottery well, and of course, she was right. It was going to be difficult to get anywhere. So, to come down here and be able to learn things and make things that could actually sell, and really be involved in something like that at that age, was really pretty amazing.

Vernon is just a really good teacher, very patient. If something really bothered him about what an apprentice was doing, he would find a very tactful way to tell you, or he would live with it himself without telling you. He's almost too nice. So, if he finally did have to tell you something, you'd be so shocked: "You didn't like something?" He never said anything that was mean.

Country Roads paid for the food. The way it was set up, twenty percent of what you made was paid to you in one lump sum at the end. As an apprentice, you brought back receipts and food was paid for. It was a really good situation. I was here when Mary and Dave Farrell got together, who are now at Westmoore Pottery.

You had so much Jugtown history ingrained in you. It did get run down for a while there. When Vernon bought it, it was like we had this whole town to keep up—but we weren't a whole town, we're two people.

I feel like we accomplish a lot together because of the different things we're interested in. He keeps the clay bodies going, and I can't tolerate bad glazes.

You have to work on each glaze, say up to ten times, changing it to get it where you want it. You go through tests, read up on it, put it through, get it out, no. Wrong direction. When you're doing glaze tests, every time you open the kiln it's like Christmas. Something new is going to come out. Something you can work with. It's a real challenge.

Employees at Jugtown Pottery, ca. 1982. Clockwise from left to right: Bob Owens, Charles Moore, Vernon Owens, Jeannette Moore, Viola Owens Brady, Pamela Lorette (Owens), and Nancy Sweezy.

Edited by Douglas DeNatale from a transcript of an interview with Pam Owens and Vernon Owens, Jugtown, North Carolina, September 30, 1993, by Sally Council.

Vernon Owens

Vernon Owens is the son of potter Melvin L. Owens. Hired by John Maré to turn pottery at Jugtown in 1959, Vernon worked through the Country Roads period of operation, and became the owner of Jugtown in 1983.

I really don't know anything about the story until 1959. I never knew that much about Jugtown until then, because I would just come down now and then and help them load the kiln or help them dig clay or that kind of thing. I still don't know that much about John Maré's background. I know that when he was a young man he was in the Navy for a few years, and that he was an antiques dealer. He had an antiques shop in Southern Pines and he owned a couple of radio stations. I don't know how long he was with Mrs. Busbee before he bought the place. I just know that he bought it from her.

Vernon Owens turning on the wheel at Jugtown, ca. 1984.

I don't understand exactly what was what, but Maré was in control of running the place and he was responsible for Mrs. Busbee's welfare. The place was tied up in court for a few months, and I think the judge ruled in his favor because Mrs. Busbee had reached the point where she wasn't able to look out for herself, and it was agreed upon that Maré would take care of her and never take her away from Jugtown. And I guess that's the reason the judge said that he was the man to have it. That would be my guess, anyway.

Maré came to me in December of 1959, and asked if I'd take a job working here. And I said, "Sure. I'll try." It was always preaching from that day on with people who were involved with the other side.

Ben and I were always friends. We never reached the point where we wouldn't speak to each other, but that feeling was always there. And it was right for him to have the feeling that he should have the place—he worked here for thirty-four years. I mean I could have gone through the same thing. I worked here for a long time for other people, and I reached a point in the late 1970s when I told Nancy and the Country Roads board that I thought it was time for me to make some decisions about whether I was going to stay on here or whether I should get out and have my own place. I could have lost everything that I put into it. So, decisions should have been made for Ben almost after Mr. Busbee died. It should have been drawn up, but it never was, and that's where they went wrong.

I guess it worked out like it was supposed to, because Ben always seemed pretty happy to be on his own and he was in control of his Pottery. Now Ben III has it, and he's got the name. It's better to have something that's handed directly to you than it is to come into something that somebody else has built. So, I guess it worked out better for all.

Maré had two problems, now that I can look back on it. He had the problem of pottery being hard to sell plus the problem of us being inexperienced. I wasn't that great a potter. I could make pots, but I wasn't that great. The quality of it was down from what it should have been, and he, not being a potter himself, he really couldn't tell me exactly what was wrong. There was a lot of bad advertisement for a few years, which kept people away from here. We had a hard time building it back up.

He was not what most people thought he was. A lot of people thought when he bought this place that he'd ruin it because he'd commercialize it. But he didn't want anything but the old traditional pottery made. He stuck with it, and he didn't live but two-and-a-half years after he bought the place. Howard Broughton was in charge of Mr. Maré's estate, and he kept running it through September of 1964, and then they decided they weren't going to keep running it, because it was taking money out of Mr. Maré's estate. So Broughton said to me, "How about if you just rent it until I can find a buyer for it," and I said, "Okay." We leased it, and Bob and I ran it for four more years, until 1968. And that's when Country Roads bought it. Nancy and I made the decisions together for years. But as far as the pottery end of it, the kiln and the clay and all that stuff, it was always my job to make it work.

It was at a bad time. That was during the Vietnam War, and the protests going on, and Nancy came and brought in outsiders and "hippy-looking" people, and the community couldn't deal with it. I was just really involved with both sides. You know, I wouldn't go through it again. That went on for two or three years, and then they began to understand that Nancy was serious about the whole thing. She was here for business. People in the area laughed about it, but I'm convinced that if the peace movement and the flower child movement hadn't happened, the pottery business would never have been revived. People thirty-five years old and up had lost interest in pottery at that time. Handmade stuff was out, nobody cared about handcrafted stuff. Then the flower children came along—"back to the earth" and all that—and it was what they wanted. And then it didn't take but a few years of them being interested before their parents got interested.

The apprenticeship program was arranged partially because Country Roads was a non-profit corporation, and part of being a non-profit corporation was to be educational. We had the idea that it worked both ways. The apprentice learned, but it was also a way for Jugtown to survive because of the apprentice being able to put labor into it without Jugtown having to pay for it with money. That's the way we survived to start with.

We started out letting them come for three months and then after we saw people were really serious about it, three months wasn't long enough for them to learn much. After that we had people staying anywhere from a month to two or three years. It worked. It worked for us, and it really worked for the apprentice. But after a while there was friction with the apprentices working alongside of Bob and me and the other people that were getting paid. I guess sometimes you are too close to something and can't see it. But it did work, and most of them, if you asked them now, they'd say it was worth what they went through because they did learn something.

Nancy and I had an influence on each other. We began to develop pottery that was more towards the individual potter instead of an original and exact reproduction of old Jugtown. I began to go away from that somewhat before she came, when I was trying to make my own stuff. But when we had to change the glazes we changed some of the shapes, too. I don't know if I had much influence on her, she'd always want my opinion when she'd make something on what I thought should be done to it. I'm sure she had ideas of what I could change on a lot of things that I made, but she never did say anything much unless I'd try to get her opinion. I guess she thought since I'd been making pottery long enough I could make it like I wanted.

The transaction from Country Roads over to me in 1983 was a very low-keyed thing. We just thought it better for

Pam Owens puts the finishing touches on a tea pot, Jugtown Pottery, ca. 1989.

the whole place. The biggest thing that happened after I bought it was that Pam and I got married. I bought it in January and we got married in May.

I couldn't have done it without Pam. Our commitment to make it work together has been the biggest thing that happened. It made a whole lot of difference. We talked about it a lot. And we've been lucky, too, we've been very lucky. I took my life's savings and put it into trying to get the place together and trying to pay the loan. We decided we just couldn't let the buildings go any more, because of the image of the place. Jugtown needs to be solid. Sometimes I feel foolish about the things I do. I think, well, maybe I should

Travis Owens, son of Vernon and Pamela Owens, works on the wheel at Jugtown, 1993.

something for a while, and if I can't see some results from it I just give up on it. She'll stay with it. I mean when she decides she going to do something, she's going to do it—something's going to give, some way or another.

One thing that we do agree on—one of the things we agree on completely is the wood-fired pottery. There's something about the quality of wood-fired pottery. You can accept pottery out of a wood kiln that you wouldn't accept out of an electric or gas kiln because you know that you're not completely in control of that pot, and that's what good about it. That's pretty much the way life is, you don't have that much control over it, and that's good. There was a time in my life that I could have made pottery without firing with wood—it's not very profitable for us compared with gas—but I have to do it now. It's part of making pottery. Two or three weeks between firing the wood kiln is just about as much as I can stand before I've got to do another. My best day is when the kiln's burning good and I'm able to just hang around the kiln and stay with the fire. If there's any satisfaction in running the place that is one part of it, being able to do that. We fire about twenty-five wood kilns a year.

I guess I look at pottery from a different angle than somebody that's come in the pottery and look at it more as art. They expect people to come to them and say, "Look at what I've done." I can't look at pottery like that. I'm always wondering why those people buy this much pottery. It's just hard for me to believe that it's possible for me to be able to make pottery and there be a demand for it. A lot of times it's really hard for me to put the price I have to have out of it, especially wood-fired pottery. Because I think, well, there

Bayle Owens, daughter of Vernon and Pamela Owens, works on the wheel at Jugtown, 1993.

might be somebody around Robbins who'd come up here and want to buy that, and they just wouldn't have that much money. I guess that's why I keep prices to where people can buy it. I'm determined that I can make pottery and put prices on it that if somebody in this community wants it, they can come up here and buy a piece of it.

save this money that I spend when I really don't have it. But when I rationalize that I know that you have to do it. Then we had Travis and that made the commitment a lot stronger, because I feel like now the place does have a possibility of being carried on within the family. And now we have Bayle. So there is a possibility that one of them will carry it on.

People walk in the shop down there and see Pam and me turning, and they think, "What a great life!" When they drive in the driveway, and see this place, they think it's ideal. And it is. But Pam and I both are people who when we decide we want something we really work at getting it done. At least half of the time that I'm in there turning pots, my mind is trying to figure out something else. For most people going into the pottery business in the last twenty years, a lot of the reason was to get out of the everyday pressure of ordinary jobs. There's been many a person who has gone in the pottery business because they say, "Well, if I can do that, I can work when I want to and take off when I want to." And there's a lot of potters in this area that do that. They close up in January. They take long vacations. And a lot of them will say, "You can do it, too—you know you can do it, too." Well, I can't do it. We can't do it. Because, you know, when you've got six people coming in to work for you, you've got to have something for them to do.

The glaze operation is Pam's thing. She has an ability to stay with something when I give up on it. I work with

Edited by Douglas DeNatale from a transcript of an interview with Vernon Owens and Pan Owens, Jugtown, North Carolina, September 30, 1992, by Sally Council.

Jugtown Personnel
═══ 1917–1994 ═══

This list should be considered a complete but not exhaustive list of personnel associated with Jugtown Pottery during its more than seventy years of operation. Over the years, the potters and the owners of Jugtown have received the majority of attention; however, as this long list suggests, Jugtown has always relied on the efforts of a much wider circle of individuals to keep it operating. The list was compiled by Pamela Owens, Vernon Owens, and Jill Severn, with the help of individuals from the Seagrove community.

1917-1959

Beginning around 1917, Jacques and Juliana Busbee acted as sales agents for local potters who worked from their own shops. In 1921 the Busbees decided to build their own pottery—Jugtown Pottery—and to hire young potters Ben Owen and Charlie Teague to turn there. The Busbee era of ownership ended in 1959.

PERSONNEL:

Jacques Busbee O G
Juliana Busbee O S
Arthur Davis *
Hurley Hussey *
Charles Moore * C
Nora Scott Moore C (worked at home)
Rancie Moore *
Ben Owen P
J. H. Owen P (never worked here made the wares at his own shop)
Martha Scott Owen C (worked at home)
Melvin Owens K
Jason Reeder *
Alice Scott C (worked at home)
Herbert Scott *
Robert Scott *
Annie Cagle Teague H
B. D. ("Duck") Teague K
Charlie Teague P
Ernest Williamson *
W. Boyce Yow * C

1959-1962

John Maré, a New York businessman and antique collector who had relocated to Southern Pines, North Carolina in the early 1950s, acquired ownership of Jugtown in 1959. He hired Vernon and Bob Owens and Charles Moore to work for him. Maré owned the pottery until 1962 when he passed away.

PERSONNEL

Steve Fludder *
John Maré O
Charles Moore * C G
Al Powers * C
Bobby Owens * G
Boyd Owens C
Melvin Owens K
Vernon Owens P C G

1962-1968

Following the death of John Maré, Vernon and Bob Owens and Charles Moore continued to operate Jugtown renting the pottery from Maré's estate through 1968.

PERSONNEL

Steve Fludder *
Charles Moore * C G
Bobby Owens * G
Boyd Owens C
Vernon Owens P C G

1968-1983

In 1968 Nancy Sweezy, one of the founders of Country Roads, a non-profit venture which promoted and marketed handicrafts, visited Jugtown Pottery and shortly thereafter arranged for Country Roads to purchase the Pottery. Together with Vernon and Bob Owens and Charles Moore, Nancy Sweezy operated Jugtown Pottery through 1983.

PERSONNEL

Agnes Chabot Almquist A P
John Almquist A P
Don Boyd *
Viola Owens Brady *
Lauri Brannon A
Kate Brown A
June Brown *
Phoebe Carter A
Peter Catazonie A
Jane Cohen A
Robert Coombs A
Leanne Cowden A
C. B. Craven P (worked at home)
Tom Crimmons A
Jenny Dowd A
Susane Dus A
Sherri Erickson A
Dave Farrell A
Mary Livingstone Farrell A
Beth Fludder *
Steve Fludder *
Carol Young Gallager A
Ivy Heyman A
Evan Jones A
Robin Jones A
Laura Keller A
Debra Knight A
Judy Levinson A
Donna Light A
Jan Mann A
Susie Marsh A
Lawrence Meade A
Cynthia Burns Monroe A
Charles Moore * C G
Jeanette Moore * S
Bob Owens * G
Pamela Lorette Owens A
Vernon Owens P C G
Rosemary Poole A C
Eric Rabinowitz A
Sharri Stevens A
Lybess Sweezy A
Lynn Sweezy A
Nancy Sweezy * P O G
Sam Sweezy *
Mary Torrey A
Susan Tunstil A
Russell Turnage A
Guy Wolff A

1983-PRESENT

Vernon Owens purchased Jugtown Pottery from Country Roads in 1983. He and his wife Pam are the current owners at Jugtown Pottery.

PERSONNEL

Dylan Bowen A
Viola Owens Brady * C
Laura Kim Brown P
Martha Cooper P
C. B. Craven P (worked at home)
Ikuko Hussey * S
Cynthia Burns Monroe P
Charles Moore * C P
Jeanette Moore * S
Bayle Owens A C
Bobby Owens * K G
Emily Owens C
Pamela Lorette Owens P C G
Travis Owens A C
Vernon Owens P C O K
Mary Praytor A
David Stuempfle P
Boyce Yow C (worked at home, catfish only)

Key to Abbreviations

*	worker
A	apprentice
P	potter
C	made chickens and animals
K	kiln builder
H	housekeeper/cook
S	sales person
G	developed glazes at Jugtown
O	owner

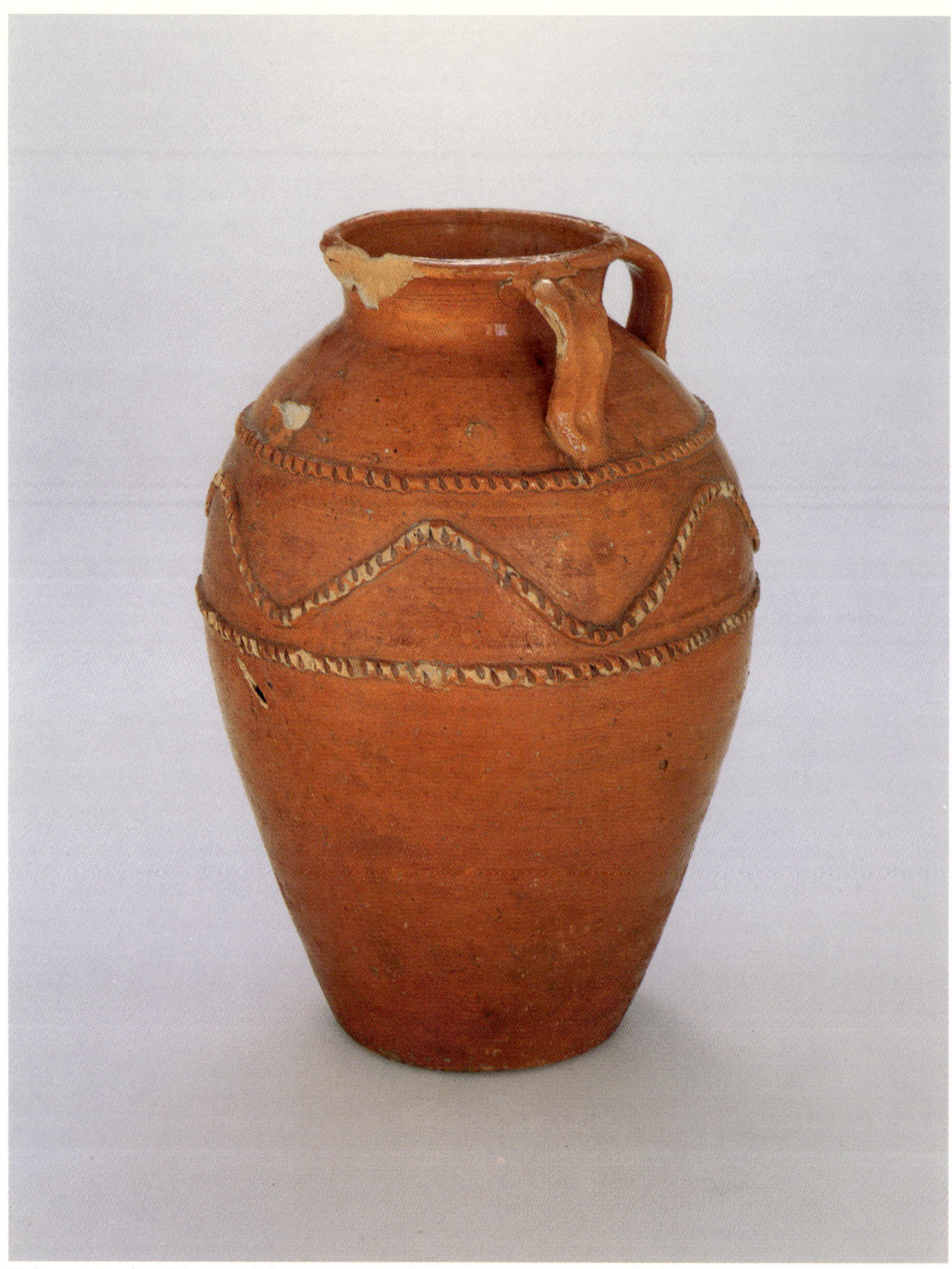

Early example of the "Persian Jar" form developed at Jugtown Pottery, ca. 1923. The form of the jar appears to be a combination of the traditional Piedmont area churn form and the oriental shapes admired by Jacques Busbee. The lead glaze used for this jar was replaced in later examples of the "Persian Jar" with the "Chinese Blue" glaze Jacques Busbee developed. Collection of Ray Wilkinson.

Catalog of Objects

Jug
Salt-glazed stoneware with incised decoration
J. D. Craven Pottery
Moore County, North Carolina
ca. 1870s
H. 10 1/2" Cir. 22 7/8"
Incised "sine wave" decoration below handle of jug and 2 incised rings at neck of the jug. Stamped next to base of handle "J. D. CRAVEN".
Ray Wilkinson

Churn with Lid
Salt-glazed stoneware
Attributed to the Auman family
Randolph County, North Carolina
ca. late 19th century
H. 17" Cir. 31 5/8"
Incised "4" below lug handle
Moore County Historical Association

Jug
Salt-glazed stoneware with incised decoration
Nicholas Fox
Chatham County, North Carolina
ca. 1850
H. 7" Cir. 16 1/2"
Decorated with 2 incised bands on shoulder of jug.
William W. Ivey

"Club Lectures/Given through The Art Department/of the/Federation of Women's Clubs of North Carolina/1915-16"
Brochure from Women's Club Speakers Bureau
ca. 1915
Illustrated
L. 9 1/2" W. 7"
Country Roads, Incorporated

The People's Art Union Historic Gallery of Portraits & Paintings/with brief memoirs of the/MOST CELEBRAT-ED MEN, of every age and country, Vol. III
Book
London: Willoughby & Company
no date
140 pages, illustrated
L. 8 5/8" W. 5 1/2"
Inscribed on the copyright page "Stolen from Jacques Busbee"
Ray Wilkinson

Fables in Slang
Book
George Ade
New York: Clyde Newman, Herbert Stone & Co., Pub.
MDCCCCI
203 pages, illustrated
L. 6 1/8" W. 4 3/8"
Inscribed on fly page "J. A. Royster May First—".
Ray Wilkinson

Flared Bowl
Southern Long Leaf Pine woven with Raffia
Nina Prim
Moore County, North Carolina
ca. 1920s-1930s
H. 4" Diam. 9 1/2"
Vivian Prim Evans

Tapered Bowl
Southern Long Leaf woven with Raffia
Nina Prim
Moore County, North Carolina
ca. 1920s-1930s
Judy Mofield Mallow

Pie Plate
Lead-glazed earthenware
Maker unknown
Randolph County, North Carolina
ca. last quarter of 19th century
H. 2 1/2" Diam. 10"
Rim of pie plate has scalloped edges. Exterior is unglazed.
William W. Ivey

Vase
Albany slip glaze stoneware
Oscar Louis Bachelder
Omar Khayyám Pottery
Buncombe County, North Carolina
ca. 1920s
H. 7" Cir. 21 1/2"
Incised monogram under the base "OLB".
George Viall

Rubáiyát of Omar Khayyám and the Salamán and Absál of Jámí: A Memorial Edition
Book
Rendered in English verse by Edward Fitzgerald
New York: Thomas Y. Crowell & Co., Publishers
288 pages with embossed gold leaf cover decoration, illustrated
L. 5 1/2" W. 4"
Inscribed on the fly page "Juliana A. Royster/July 16, 1903".
Ray Wilkinson

Pitcher
Salt-glazed stoneware with cobalt decoration
Maker unknown
ca. 1917
H. 7 1/2" Cir. 17 3/4"
Incised "sine wave" decoration with cobalt around collar and belly of pitcher. Interior of pitcher and handle covered with cobalt slip.
Moore County Historical Association

Vase
Salt-glazed stoneware with slip, incising, and rouletting
J. H. Owen, possibly for Jugtown Pottery
Moore County, North Carolina
ca. 1917
H. 8" Cir. 22 3/4"
Incised "sine wave" decoration below the shoulder. Four bands of impressed "rouletting" made by coggle wheel. Cobalt slip applied on the rim and above shoulder of vase.
The Wilkinson Collection

Bowl
Salt-glazed stoneware with slip, incising, and rouletting
J. H. Owen, for Jugtown Pottery
Moore County, North Carolina
ca. 1917-1923
H. 7" Cir. 32 5/8"
Interior of bowl covered with cobalt slip. Band of impressed "rouletting" just below the rim. Incised "sine wave" decoration with cobalt slip swirls below rouletting.
The Wilkinson Collection

Standard Test Lessons in Reading, Book Five [Practice Lessons For Grades 5, 6, or 7]
Educational Pamphlet
Prepared by William A. McCall and Lelah Mae Crabbs
New York: Bureau of Publications, Teacher's College, Columbia University
1926
L. 15" W. 10 1/4"
Mounted on cardboard and laminated with clear plastic
Country Roads, Incorporated

Rousseau and Romanticism
Book
Irving Babbitt
New York: Houghton Mifflin
1919
426 pages, illustrated
L. 8 1/2" W. 5 7/8"
Inscribed on the fly page "Juliana R. Busbee/July 1919"
Ray Wilkinson

The Poems of Oscar Wilde, vol. 1
Book
Oscar Wilde
New York: F. M. Buckles & Co.
1906
151 pages

L. 7 3/4" W. 5 1/4"
Inscribed on fly page "J. Royster/1907"
Ray Wilkinson

Dome-lidded Tea Pot
Salt-glazed stoneware with cobalt blue decoration
Ben Owen, Jugtown Pottery
Moore County, North Carolina
ca. 1921-1959
H. 6 1/2" Cir. 19 5/8"
Cobalt slip "swirl" decoration around the shoulder of the tea pot and on the lid. Stamped under the base "JUGTOWN WARE".
Pamela and Vernon Owens

Dome-lidded Sugar Bowl
Salt-glazed stoneware with cobalt blue and incised decoration
Ben Owen, Jugtown Pottery
Moore County, North Carolina
ca. 1921-1959
H. 4 3/4" Cir. 13 1/2"
Cobalt slip "swirl" decoration around the shoulder of the bowl, the lid, and the handles. Stamped under the base "JUGTOWN WARE".
Pamela and Vernon Owens

Cream Pitcher
Salt-glazed stoneware with cobalt blue and incised decoration
Ben Owen, Jugtown Pottery
Moore County, North Carolina
ca. 1921-1959
H. 4 1/2" Cir. 12 1/2"
Cobalt slip "swirl" decoration on base of spout. Stamped under the base "JUGTOWN WARE".
Pamela and Vernon Owens

Jar
Salt-glazed stoneware with incised and slip decoration
J. H. Owen, for Jugtown Pottery
Moore County, North Carolina
ca. 1919
H. 18 1/2" Cir. 36"
Incised "sine wave" pattern with areas of cobalt and iron slip between the handles.
Pamela and Vernon Owens

"Double-Gourd Vase"
Salt-glazed stoneware with copper slip decoration
Ben Owen, Jugtown Pottery
Moore County, North Carolina
ca. 1920s
H. 7 1/4" Cir. 12"
Copper slip on rim of vase flowing over shoulder. Stamped under the base "JUGTOWN WARE".
Leonidas J. Betts

Candlestick
Salt-glazed stoneware with incised and slip decorations
J. H. Owen, for Jugtown Pottery
Moore County, North Carolina
ca. early 1920s
H. 9" Cir. 12 1/4"
Incised "sine wave" pattern around base with cobalt slip.
Cobalt slip band around upper edge of collar.
Daniel Ray Owen

Cup
"Tobacco Spit" glaze earthenware
Ben Owen, Jugtown Pottery
Moore County, North Carolina
ca. 1921-1959
H. 2 1/4" Cir. 11 1/4"
Stamped under the base "JUGTOWN WARE".
Salem Academy and College

Bread Plate
"Tobacco Spit" glaze earthenware
Ben Owen, Jugtown Pottery
Moore County, North Carolina
ca. 1921-1959
H. 3/4" Diam. 6"
Stamped under the base "JUGTOWN WARE".
Salem Academy and College

Dinner Plate
"Tobacco Spit" glaze earthenware
Ben Owen, Jugtown Pottery
Moore County, North Carolina
ca. 1921-1959
H. 1 1/4" Diam. 10 1/2"
Stamped under the base "JUGTOWN WARE".
Salem Academy and College

"Confederate Cup"
Lead-glazed stoneware
Ben Owen, Jugtown Pottery
Moore County, North Carolina
ca. 1930s-1940s
H. 3" Cir. 14 1/4"
Stamped under the base "JUGTOWN WARE".
Salem Academy and College

"Chicken Pie Plate"
Lead-glazed earthenware with slip decoration
Ben Owen or Charlie Teague, Jugtown Pottery
Moore County, North Carolina
ca. 1920s-1930s
H. 2 1/4" Diam. 10 1/2"
Yellow slip chicken painted on the interior of the pie plate.
Stamped under the base "JUGTOWN WARE".
McKissick Museum, The University of South Carolina

Egg Basket
Woven split oak
Maker unknown
North Carolina
ca. early 1920s
H. 17" Diam. 13"
Pamela and Vernon Owens

Basket
Woven split oak with vegetable dye decoration
Maker unknown
North Carolina
ca. early 1920s
H. 13 1/2" Diam. 8 3/4"
Pamela and Vernon Owens

Overshot Coverlet
Wool and cotton with an overshot weave
Maker unknown
Moore County, North Carolina
ca. 1850-1900
L. 78" W. 64"
Coverlet consists of two loom widths that have been
whip-stitched together.
Owen Collins

**American History and Travel/including the/North Carolina
Collection/of Jacques Busbee/with many/Rare and Desirable
Books/ To be sold at Auction/ FRIDAY AFTERNOON,
JULY 1, 1921/commencing at 2:30 o'clock.**
Auction Catalog Pamphlet
New York: The Walpole Galleries
1921
L. 8 1/2" W 5 3/4"
Country Roads, Incorporated

Strap-handle Platter
"Accidental" lead-glazed earthenware
Ben Owen or Charlie Teague, Jugtown Pottery
Moore County, North Carolina
ca. 1920s
H. 3" Diam. 14"
Stamped under the base "JUGTOWN WARE".
Daniel Ray Owen

"Persian Jar"
Lead-glazed earthenware with applied clay decoration
Ben Owen, Jugtown Pottery
Moore County, North Carolina
ca. 1923
H. 16" Cir. 36 1/2"
Decorated with two straight "rope" clay bands on shoulder
with one "rope" clay band looped between in a "sine wave"
pattern. No stamp.
Ray Wilkinson

"Accidental" lead-glazed earthenware candlesticks [left] by Charlie Teague at Jugtown, ca. 1920s. Occasionally, when lead-glazed wares were fired in the wood kiln, the orange color of the wares would be mottled with spots of green. Juliana Busbee loved this effect, dubbing it "Accidental" glaze. "Frogskin" glaze stoneware pitcher [right] by Ben Owen at Jugtown, ca. 1930s. "Frogskin" glaze—Albany slip glaze with salt added to it during firing—was first introduced into the Seagrove area in the late 19th century by potter, J. D. Craven. Later on, Jugtown adopted "Frogskin" as one of its primary glazes. Both are from the collection of Pamela and Vernon Owens.

Platter
Lead-glazed earthenware with yellow slip decoration
Ben Owen, Jugtown Pottery
Moore County, North Carolina
ca. 1930s
H. 1 1/4" Diam. 16"
Decorated on center of platter with yellow slip shield with bear motif. Stamped under the base "JUGTOWN WARE".
William W. Ivey

Jar
Experimental glaze (red and blue) stoneware
Ben Owen or Charlie Teague, Jugtown Pottery
Moore County, North Carolina
ca. 1920s
H. 7 1/2" Cir. 19 1/4"
Incised "X" on the base to indicate that it was a glaze test piece. Stamped under the base "JUGTOWN WARE".
Ray Wilkinson

Jar
Experimental glaze (green, purple, white) stoneware
Ben Owen or Charlie Teague, Jugtown Pottery
Moore County, North Carolina
ca. 1920s
H. 7 1/2" Cir. 18"
Stamped under the base "JUGTOWN WARE".
Ray Wilkinson

Chalice
Early example of "Chinese Blue" glaze stoneware
Ben Owen or Charlie Teague , Jugtown Pottery
Moore County, North Carolina
ca. 1920s
H. 6" Cir. 11 1/2"
Stamped under the base "JUGTOWN WARE".
Donald and Betty Morphis

Vase
"Chinese Red" glaze stoneware
Jonah Owens, North State Pottery Company
Chatham (Lee) County, North Carolina
ca. 1925
H. 10" Cir. 21 3/4"
Stamped under the base "NORTH STATE POTTERY CO./ HAND MADE/ SANFORD, N. C."
Leonidas J. Betts

Bowl
"Chinese Blue" glaze stoneware
Ben Owen, Jugtown Pottery
Moore County, North Carolina
ca. 1921-1959
H. 4" Cir. 20 3/4"
Stamped under the base "JUGTOWN WARE".
McKissick Museum, The University of South Carolina

Vase
Yellow glaze stoneware with cobalt slip decoration
Auman Pottery
Randolph County, North Carolina
ca. early 1920s
H. 5" Cir. 23 3/4"
Cobalt slip on both handles and around shoulder of vase with drips flowing down the side of the vase.
The Wilkinson Collection

Pitcher
Chrome-red glaze earthenware with incised initials
Waymon Cole, J. B. Cole Pottery for
Sunset Mountain Gift Shop
Montgomery County, North Carolina
ca. 1935
H. 10" Cir. 23 5/8"
Incised on belly of the pitcher "W/C"
William W. Ivey

"Rebekah Pitcher"
"Mirror Black" glaze earthenware
J. B. Cole Pottery
Montgomery County, North Carolina
ca. 1928
H. 11 1/2" Cir. 18 1/4"
Stamped under the base "J. B. COLE/Pottery/ STEEDS, N. C."
William W. Ivey

Vase
Light-green glaze earthenware with 3 decorative handles
J. B. Cole Pottery
Montgomery County, North Carolina
ca. 1928
H. 5 1/2" Cir. 24 1/4"
Stamped under the base "J. B. COLE/Pottery/ STEEDS, N. C."
The Wilkinson Collection

Vase
Light-blue glaze earthenware with 3 decorative handles
J. B. Cole Pottery for Sunset Mountain Gift Shop
Montgomery County, North Carolina
ca. 1935
H. 6 1/2" Cir. 17"
Stamped under the base "SUNSET/MOUNTAIN/ POTTERY".
The Wilkinson Collection

Dome-lidded Cracker Jar
"Mirror Black" glaze earthenware
Walter Owen, North State Pottery
Lee County, North Carolina
1925-1939
H. 9" Cir. 18 1/2"
Stamped under the base "North State Pottery Co./ Hand Made/Sanford N. C."
McKissick Museum, The University of South Carolina

Strap-handled Platter
Lead-glazed earthenware
Ben Owen, Jugtown Pottery
Moore County, North Carolina
ca. 1930s
H. 3" Diam. 14"
Stamped under the base "JUGTOWN WARE".
Pamela and Vernon Owens

Pitcher
"Frogskin" glaze stoneware
Ben Owen, Jugtown Pottery
Moore County, North Carolina
ca. 1930s
H. 9 1/4" Cir. 26 7/8"
Stamped under the base "JUGTOWN WARE".
Pamela and Vernon Owens

Chalice
Lead-glazed earthenware
Ben Owen, Jugtown Pottery
Moore County, North Carolina
ca. 1930s
H. 6" Cir. 10 3/4"
Stamped under the base "JUGTOWN WARE".
Courtesy of The Visual Arts Center
North Carolina State University
Leonidas J. Betts Collection
984.9.64

"Fox Jug"
Salt-glazed stoneware with incised decoration
Ben Owen, Jugtown Pottery
Moore County, North Carolina
ca. 1923-1959
H. 9 1/2" Cir. 23 1/2"
Three incised bands across body of vessel. Stamped under the base "JUGTOWN WARE".
Collection of St. John's Museum of Art, Wilmington, NC,
Gift of Woodrow W. Pruett and William S. Bridges in memory of Juliana Royster Busbee

Miniature Jug
Salt-glazed stoneware
Ben Owen, Jugtown Pottery
Moore County, North Carolina
ca. 1923-1959
H. 4 1/2" Cir. 15"
Two incised rings on upper shoulder. Stamped under the base "JUGTOWN WARE".
Collection of St. John's Museum of Art, Wilmington, NC,
Gift of Woodrow W. Pruett and William S. Bridges in memory of Juliana Royster Busbee

Wine Bottle

Salt-glazed stoneware with incised band and slip decoration.
Ben Owen, Jugtown Pottery
Moore County, North Carolina
ca. 1923-1959
H. 7 1/2" Cir. 23 1/4"
Incised band around shoulder with iron slip decoration on band and mouth. Two "dogwood" motifs applied between neck and shoulder.
Stamped under the base "JUGTOWN WARE".
Salem Academy and College

Dome-lidded Tureen
"Tobacco Spit" glaze earthenware
Ben Owen, Jugtown Pottery
Moore County, North Carolina
ca. 1930s
H. 7 3/4" Cir. 31 1/4"
Stamped under the base "JUGTOWN WARE".
Pamela and Vernon Owens

Dome-lidded Cracker Jar
Lead-glazed earthenware
Ben Owen, Jugtown Pottery
Moore County, North Carolina
ca. 1923-1959
H. 10" Cir. 24 3/4"
Stamped under the base "JUGTOWN WARE".
Salem Academy and College

"Oriental Jar"
"Mirror Black" glaze earthenware with applied clay attachments
Ben Owen, Jugtown Pottery
Moore County, North Carolina
ca. 1935-1945
H. 12 1/2" Cir. 36"
Two clay "dogwood" motifs applied above shoulder of vase.
Stamped under the base "JUGTOWN WARE".
George Viall

"Dogwood Vase"
White glaze stoneware with applied clay decoration
Ben Owen, Jugtown Pottery
Moore County, North Carolina
ca. 1950s
H. 13 1/4" Cir. 23"
Two applied "dogwood" motifs at shoulder of jar. Stamped under the base "JUGTOWN WARE".
Pamela and Vernon Owens

"Lily Vase"
White glaze stoneware
Ben Owen, Jugtown Pottery
Moore County, North Carolina
ca. 1930s
H. 10" Cir. 23 1/4"
Stamped under the base "JUGTOWN WARE".
Pamela and Vernon Owens

"Egg Vase"

"Egg Vase"
"Chinese Blue" glaze stoneware
Ben Owen, Jugtown Pottery
Moore County, North Carolina
ca. 1930s-1959
H. 6 1/2" Cir. 14 1/2"
Stamped under the base "JUGTOWN WARE".
Collection of St. John's Museum of Art, Wilmington, NC,
Gift of Woodrow W. Pruett and William S. Bridges in memory
of Juliana Royster Busbee

"Korean Bowl"
"Chinese Blue" glaze stoneware
Ben Owen, Jugtown Pottery
Moore County, North Carolina
ca. 1930s-1947
H. 3" Cir. 26 1/4"
Stamped under the base "JUGTOWN WARE".
Moore County Historical Association

"Chinese Jar"
"Chinese Blue" glaze stoneware
Ben Owen, Jugtown Pottery
Moore County, North Carolina
ca. 1930s-1947
H. 6 1/2" Cir. 17"
Stamped under the base "JUGTOWN WARE".
Salem Academy and College

"Han Vase"
"Chinese Blue" glaze stoneware
Ben Owen, Jugtown Pottery
Moore County, North Carolina
ca. 1930s-1947
H. 8 3/4" Cir. 26"
Stamped under the base "JUGTOWN WARE".
Country Roads, Incorporated

**"Jugtown Ware/AN/AMERICAN CRAFT/WITH/A
PEDIGREE/BY WAY OF A CATALOG"**
Pamphlet
Jacques Busbee
Steeds, N.C.: Jugtown Pottery
ca.1943
Illustrated
L. 7 1/2" W. 3 1/2"
Joanne Bluethenthal

"THE GENESIS of/ JUGTOWN"
Pamphlet
Juliana Busbee
Reprint from *Bulletin of the American Ceramic Society*
Seagrove, N.C.: Jugtown Pottery
October, 1937
8 pages
L. 5 1/2" W. 3 1/2"
Joanne Bluethenthal

Punch Bowl
"Chinese Blue" glaze stoneware
Ben Owen, Jugtown Pottery
Moore County, North Carolina
ca. 1930s-1940s
H. 7" Cir. 42"
Stamped under the base "JUGTOWN WARE".
Moore County Historical Association

Large Chicken Shaker
"Accidental" lead-glazed earthenware with incised marks and
slip decoration
Attributed to Juliana Busbee, Jugtown Pottery
Moore County, North Carolina
ca. 1940s-1950s
H. 8 3/4" Cir. 17"
Chicken features incised on form. Slip decoration on head,
back, and tail.
Collection of St. John's Museum of Art, Wilmington, NC,
Gift of Woodrow W. Pruett and William S. Bridges in memory
of Juliana Royster Busbee

"Dogwood Bowl"
Salt-glazed stoneware with white slip decoration
Ben Owen, Jugtown Pottery
Moore County, North Carolina
ca. 1940s-1959
H. 4 3/4" Cir. 31"
White slip "dogwood" motif on the interior surface of the
bowl. Stamped under the base "JUGTOWN WARE".
Country Roads, Incorporated

"Chinese Bulb Bowl"
White glaze stoneware
Ben Owen, Jugtown Pottery
Moore County, North Carolina
ca. 1930s-1959
H. 5 1/4" Cir. 22 3/8"
Stamped under the base "JUGTOWN WARE".
Collection of St. John's Museum of Art, Wilmington, NC,
Gift of Woodrow W. Pruett and William S. Bridges in memory
of Juliana Royster Busbee

Bean Pot with Lid
Lead-glazed earthenware
Ben Owen, Jugtown Pottery
Moore County, North Carolina
ca. 1930s-1940s
H. 7 1/2" Cir. 26"
Stamped under the base "JUGTOWN WARE".
Pamela and Vernon Owens

"Persian Jar" in "Chinese Blue" glaze, by Ben Owen at Jugtown, ca. 1930s. An example of the mature form and glaze of the Jugtown "Persian Jar." Collection of Moore County Historical Association.

Lead-glazed earthenware
Attributed to Alice Scott, for Jugtown Pottery
Moore County, North Carolina
ca. 1930s-1945
H. 4 1/4" Cir. 7"
Collection of St. John's Museum of Art, Wilmington, NC,
Gift of Woodrow W. Pruett and William S. Bridges in memory
of Juliana Royster Busbee

Catfish Sculpture
"Frogskin" glaze stoneware
W. Boyce Yow, for Jugtown Pottery
Moore County, North Carolina
H. 2 1/2" L. 11 1/4" Cir. 6"
Within impressed ring on underside of fish "W. BOYCE/YOW" (formed by series of punctates). "SEAGROVE N.C." (formed by series of punctates) also on underside of fish.
Courtesy of The Visual Arts Center
North Carolina State University
Leonidas J. Betts Collection
1991.22.32

Candlesticks [pair]
"Accidental" lead-glazed earthenware
Charlie Teague, Jugtown Pottery
Moore County, North Carolina
ca. 1920s
H. 8 1/2" Cir. 11 1/2"
Both are stamped under the base "JUGTOWN".
Pamela and Vernon Owens

Bowl
Lead-glazed earthenware with incised decoration
Charlie Teague, Jugtown Pottery
Moore County, North Carolina
ca. 1920s
H. 6 1/2" Cir. 33"
Incised "sine wave" decoration on exterior of bowl. Stamped under the base "JUGTOWN WARE".
Ray Wilkinson

"Persian Jar"
"Chinese Blue" glaze stoneware with incised and applied
clay decorations
Ben Owen, Jugtown Pottery
Moore County, North Carolina
ca. 1930s
H. 17 1/2" Cir. 38 7/8"
Two incised lines at shoulder of jar. Attached clay "rope" decoration looped between lines in "sine wave" pattern. Stamped under the base "JUGTOWN WARE".
Moore County Historical Association

"Soul Jar"
Salt-glazed stoneware with carved band and slip decoration
Ben Owen, Jugtown Pottery
Moore County, North Carolina
ca. 1923-1959
H. 8 3/4" Cir. 32 5/8"
Band of carved decoration around shoulder with iron slip border above and below the band. Stamped under the base "JUGTOWN WARE".
Collection of St. John's Museum of Art, Wilmington, NC,
Gift of Woodrow W. Pruett and William S. Bridges in memory
of Juliana Royster Busbee

"JUGTOWN/JACQUES BUSBEE 1873-1947"
Exhibition Pamphlet
Raleigh, N.C.: North Carolina State Art Society, Isabelle Bowen Henderson, Chair
4 pages, illustrated
L. 9" W. 6"
Country Roads, Incorporated

Jugtown Pottery
Book
Jean Crawford
Winston-Salem: John F. Blair, Publisher
1964
127 pages, illustrated
L. 9 1/4" W. 8"
McKissick Museum, The University of South Carolina

Dome-lidded Casserole
Lead-glazed stoneware
Vernon Owens, Jugtown Pottery
Moore County, North Carolina
ca. early 1960s
H. 8 3/4" Cir. 43"
Stamped under the base "JUGTOWN WARE".
Pamela and Vernon Owens

Pie Plate
Lead-glazed stoneware
Vernon Owens, Jugtown Pottery
Moore County, North Carolina
ca. early 1960s
H. 2 1/4" Diam. 9 1/4"
Stamped under the base "JUGTOWN WARE".
William W. Ivey

Plate
Lead-glazed earthenware
Vernon Owens, Jugtown Pottery
Moore County, North Carolina
ca. early 1960s
H. 1 1/4" Diam. 8 1/2"
Stamped under the base "JUGTOWN WARE".
Leonidas J. Betts

Candlesticks [Pair]
Salt-glazed stoneware with cobalt slip decoration
Vernon Owens, Jugtown Pottery
Moore County, North Carolina
ca. early 1960s.
H. 8" Cir. 12 5/8"
Both are stamped under the base "JUGTOWN WARE"
with a wedge-shaped impression surrounding stamp. Both
have cobalt slip decoration around the base.
Stephen and Lala Compton

1973 Price Sheet
Single sheet heavy card stock printed on both sides
Seagrove, N.C.: Jugtown Pottery
1973
1 page
L. 11" W. 8 1/4"
Joanne Bluethenthal

Punch Bowl
Salt-glazed stoneware
Vernon Owens, Jugtown Pottery
Moore County, North Carolina
1978
H. 7 5/8" Cir. 50 5/8"
Incised under the base "Made by Vernon Owens, Saturday
March 4, 1978, was a cold windy day".
Peggy and Jack Kenealy

Pitcher
"Frogskin" glaze stoneware
Vernon Owens, Jugtown Pottery
Moore County, North Carolina
1975
H. 7 1/4" Cir. 17 3/4"
Incised under the base "Vernon/Owens/1975/Moore
County/N.C."
Leonidas J. Betts

Coffee Pot
White glaze stoneware
Vernon Owens, Jugtown Pottery
Moore County, North Carolina
1978
H. 6 1/2" Cir. 20 1/2"
Stamped under the base "JUGTOWN WARE/1978".
Leonidas J. Betts

Bean Pot
"Tobacco Spit" glaze earthenware
Vernon Owens, Jugtown Pottery
Moore County, North Carolina
ca. 1968-1975
H. 6" Cir. 20"
Stamped under the base "JUGTOWN WARE".
Charles Tompkins

Stoppered Jug
Salt-glazed with cobalt and iron slip decoration
Vernon Owens, Jugtown Pottery
Moore County, North Carolina
1976
H. 10" Cir. 23 5/8"
Decorated on belly surface with cobalt and iron slip bird on
branch. Stamped under the base "JUGTOWN WARE"
and incised under the base "1976".
Pamela and Vernon Owens

Vase
Experimental copper glaze stoneware
Vernon Owens, Jugtown Pottery
Moore County, North Carolina
ca. 1970s
H. 9 3/8" Cir. 20 1/2"
Stamped under the base "JUGTOWN WARE".
Mark and Yolanda Kutney

Vase
"Black Ankle" glaze stoneware
Vernon Owens, Jugtown Pottery
Moore County, North Carolina
ca. 1973-1974
H. 4 1/4" Cir. 16 5/8"
Stamped under the base "JUGTOWN WARE".
Anne and Allen Bloom

"Neck Vase"
"Black Ankle" glaze stoneware
Vernon Owens, Jugtown Pottery
Moore County, North Carolina
ca. 1969-1970
H. 10 1/4" Cir. 21 3/4"
Stamped under the base "JUGTOWN WARE".
William W. Ivey

Glaze Tester Bowl
Blue glaze stoneware
Nancy Sweezy, Jugtown Pottery
Moore County, North Carolina
ca. 1970s
H. 2 1/4" Cir. 14 1/4"
McKissick Museum, The University of South Carolina

Glaze Tester Bowl
Alkaline-glazed stoneware
Nancy Sweezy, Jugtown Pottery
Moore County, North Carolina
ca. 1970s
H. 2 1/4" Cir. 14 3/8"
McKissick Museum, The University of South Carolina

This salt-glazed stoppered jug with painted bird was made by Vernon Owens at Jugtown, ca. 1970s. This was one of several new forms developed at Jugtown by Vernon Owens and Nancy Sweezy during the Country Roads period of operation. Collection of Pamela and Vernon Owens.

Stoneware "Neck Vase" [left] with an experimental glaze combination of "Claire de lune" and Albany slip by Pamela Owens at Jugtown, 1993. Stoneware jar [right] in "Peach Bloom" glaze, by Vernon Owens at Jugtown, 1989. Collection of Pamela and Vernon Owens.

Cake Pan
"Blue Ridge Blue" glaze stoneware
Vernon Owens, Jugtown Pottery
Moore County, North Carolina
1983
H. 4 1/2" Cir. 33 1/8"
Stamped under the base "JUGTOWN WARE/1983" and incised "Vernon/Owens".
Charles Tompkins

Colander
Feldspathic glaze (brown) stoneware
Pamela Lorette, Jugtown Pottery
Moore County, North Carolina
1981
H. 4 1/2" Cir. 27 3/4"
Stamped under the base "JUGTOWN WARE/1981".
Pamela and Vernon Owens

"Spoon Jar"
White glaze stoneware with incised decoration
Cynthia Burns, Jugtown Pottery
Moore County, North Carolina
1980
H. 4 1/2" Cir. 13 1/4"
Incised leaf and branch decoration on one side. Stamped under the base "JUGTOWN WARE/1980". Incised in script "Cynthia/Burns".
Pamela and Vernon Owens

Small Bundt Pan
"Wood Smoke" glaze earthenware
Agnes Chabot, Jugtown Pottery
Moore County, North Carolina
1973
H. 3 1/4" Cir. 22 1/2"
Incised under the base "Agnes-Chabot-'73".
Pamela and Vernon Owens

"Persian Jar"
"Chinese Blue" glaze stoneware with applied clay decoration
Vernon Owens, Jugtown Pottery
Moore County, North Carolina
1989
H. 16 1/2" Cir. 35"
Two incised lines at shoulder of jar. Attached clay "rope" decoration looped between incised lines in "sine wave" pattern. Stamped under the base "JUGTOWN WARE/1989" and incised under the base "Vernon Owens".
Pamela and Vernon Owens

Jar
Alkaline-glazed stoneware with carved decoration
Vernon Owens, Jugtown Pottery
Moore County, North Carolina
1992
H. 13 1/4" Cir. 33 1/8"
Stamped under the base "JUGTOWN WARE" and incised "Vernon/Owens/1992". Upper shoulder has three carved clay bands. Lower 2/3 of exterior of jar are unglazed.
Leonidas J. Betts

Vase
"Peach Bloom" glaze stoneware
Vernon Owens, Jugtown Pottery
Moore County, North Carolina
1989
H. 10 3/4" Cir. 22 1/8"
Stamped under the base "JUGTOWN WARE/1989" and incised on bottom "Vernon/Owens".
Pamela and Vernon Owens

Candlesticks [pair]
Salt-glazed stoneware
Vernon Owens, Jugtown Pottery
Moore County, North Carolina
1983
H. 17 1/2" Cir. 16"
Incised on the bottom "Vernon Owens". Stamped under the base "JUGTOWN WARE/1983".
Courtesy of The Visual Arts Center
North Carolina State University
The Leonidas J. Betts Collection
1991.22.2

"Oriental Jar"
Salt-glazed stoneware with decorative strap handles
Vernon Owens, Jugtown Pottery
Moore County, North Carolina
1987
H. 10" Cir. 23"
Stamped on the foot "VERNON OWENS" and on the bottom "JUGTOWN WARE". Incised on the bottom "Vernon Owens"
Leonidas J. Betts

Churn with Lid
Salt-glazed stoneware
Vernon Owens, Jugtown Pottery
Moore County, North Carolina
1987
H. 12 1/2" Cir. 27 3/4"
Incised on upper shoulder "sine-wave" decoration. Stamped under the base "JUGTOWN WARE/VERNON OWENS/1987".
Pamela and Vernon Owens

"Dragon Jar"
"Claire-de-lune" glaze stoneware with applied clay decoration
Vernon Owens, Jugtown Pottery
Moore County, North Carolina
1993
H. 15 1/4" Cir. 24 1/4"
Two "dragon's head" motifs applied at shoulder of jar.
Stamped under the base "JUGTOWN WARE/1993" and
incised "Vernon Owens".
Pamela and Vernon Owens

"Neck Vase"
Experimental Albany slip and "Claire-de-lune" glaze stoneware
Pamela Owens, Jugtown Pottery
Moore County, North Carolina
1993
H. 8 1/2" Cir. 20 1/4"
Stamped under the base "JUGTOWN WARE/1993" and
incised "Pamela Owens".
Pamela and Vernon Owens

Miniature Jug
Salt-glazed stoneware with incised decoration
Pamela Owens, Jugtown Pottery
Moore County, North Carolina
1986
H. 6 1/8" Cir. 16"
Two incised rings at neck of jug. Stamped under the base
"JUGTOWN WARE/1986" and incised signature "Pamela
Owens" on the base.
Leonidas J. Betts

Jug
Salt-glazed stoneware with incised "bird-fish" motif and verse
Pamela Owens, Jugtown Pottery
Moore County, North Carolina
1993
Incised parallel lines on the upper shoulder and lip. Incised
bird-fish motif on one side of vessel and incised verse "I like
Southern pots. I married Vernon Owens/But I'm kin to
Daniel Goodale/Through my mother in the North/A
Southern potter I've become and so I must toil/My clay it
comes from the Southern soil/Pamela Goodale Lorette
Owens". Stamped under the base "JUGTOWN WARE".
H. 10 1/4" Cir. 22 5/8"
Pamela and Vernon Owens

Pitcher
Salt-glazed stoneware
Charlie Craven, for Jugtown Pottery
Moore County, North Carolina
1988
H. 11" Cir. 23 1/4"
Stamped under the base "JUGTOWN WARE/1988/C.B.
Craven".
Pamela and Vernon Owens

Chicken Sculpture
Salt-glazed stoneware with iron wash
Charles Moore, Jugtown Pottery
Moore County, North Carolina
1984
H. 8" Cir. 15"
Stamped twice under the base "JUGTOWN WARE".
Incised under the base "Charles Moore/1991".
Courtesy of The Visual Arts Center
North Carolina State University
Leonidas J. Betts Collection
1991.22.36

**"Important Southern Folk Pottery/at/Absentee
Auction/the collections of/Kate and Ralph
Rinzler/and/Country Roads, Inc./Nancy Sweezy"**
Auction catalog
Seagrove, N.C.: Presented by The Southern Folk Pottery
Collectors Society
1993
90 pages, illustrated
L. 11" W. 8 1/2"
McKissick Museum, The University of South Carolina

Pottery Shop Guide/For/Seagrove Area
Guide
Compiled by William W. Ivey, illus. Dot Kimelman
Seagrove, N.C.: Friends of N.C. Pottery Museum
November, 1993
16 pages illustrated, fold out map
Friends of N.C. Pottery Museum

Dome-lidded Cracker Jar
"Tobacco Spit" glaze earthenware
Ben Owen III, Ben Owen Pottery
Moore County, North Carolina
1986
H. 12" Cir. 26"
Incised under the base "Ben Owen III/ 1986"
Courtesy of The Visual Arts Center
North Carolina State University
Leonidas J. Betts Collection
1991.22.99a,b

"Persian Jar"
"Chinese Blue" glaze stoneware
Ben Owen III, Ben Owen Pottery
Moore County, North Carolina
1988
H. 14 1/4" Cir. 30 5/8"
Incised under the base "Ben/Owen/III/1988".
Leonidas J. Betts

"Sung Jar," ash-glazed with areas of rutile slip applied with an airbrush. Surface is covered with incised vertical lines, by Ben Owen III at Ben Owen Pottery, 1993. Collection of Ben Owen III.

Candlesticks [pair]
Salt-glazed stoneware
Ben Owen III, Ben Owen Pottery
Moore County, North Carolina
1992
H. 11 1/4" Cir. 14 1/4"
Incised under the base "Ben Owen III 1992".
Ben Owen III

"Melon Jar"
"Timaku" glaze stoneware
Ben Owen III, Ben Owen Pottery
Moore County, North Carolina
1993
H. 11" Cir. 23 1/2"
Incised under the base "Ben/Owen/III/1993".
Ben Owen III

"Sung Jar"
Ash-glazed stoneware with incised vertical grooves and three loop handles
Ben Owen III, Ben Owen Pottery
Moore County, North Carolina
1993
H. 11 1/8" Cir. 25"
Incised under the base "Ben/Owen/III/1993".
Ben Owen III

"T'ang Jar"
"Chinese Blue" glaze stoneware
Ben Owen III, Ben Owen Pottery
Moore County, North Carolina
1991
H. 7 1/4" Cir. 17 1/4"
Incised under the base "Ben/Owen/III/1991".
Ben Owen III

Face Jug
Salt-glazed stoneware with applied clay facial features
Travis Owen, Jugtown Pottery
Moore County, North Carolina
1992
H. 5 3/4" Cir. 17"
Incised under the base "1992/Jug by/Pam Owens/Face/by/Travis".
Pamela and Vernon Owens

Face Jug
Salt-glazed stoneware with applied clay facial features
Decorated by Bayle Owen, Jugtown Pottery
Moore County, North Carolina
1990
H. 3 1/2" Cir. 9 5/8"
Incised under the base "Bayle's/1rst/Face Jug/5-1-90".
Pamela and Vernon Owens

Dome-lidded Sugar Jar
Clear glaze earthenware with slip decoration
Dave Farrell, Westmoore Pottery
Moore County, North Carolina
1994
H. 11 1/4" Cir. 25 1/2"
Repeating lines of colored slip decoration in green, white, and black. Incised under the base "D. Farrell/Westmoore/Pottery /1994".
Dave and Mary Farrell, Westmoore Pottery

Cream Pitcher
Blue glaze earthenware
Nell Cole Graves, J. B. Cole Pottery
Montgomery County, North Carolina
1993
H. 4 1/2" Cir. 17"
Incised under the base "93/J B ColES/SEAGROVE NC/NELL COLE/GRAVES/AGE 84".
Charles Jackson Barber, Jr.

Shirt dress
Blue and black embroidered cream silk pongee
American
ca. 1922
The Museum at the Fashion Institute of Technology
Gift of Mrs. Cora Ginsburg

New Ways *for* Old Jugs

The typefaces used in this book are Adobe Garamond,
Garamond 3 Small Caps & Old Style Figures,
and Bauer Bodoni Old Style Figures.

This book was designed by Lyn Bell Rose,
with production assistance provided by Tracey Thompson.